From Overdraft To Overflow

3 Steps to Possession in a Recession

D<small>AWN</small> J<small>OYNER</small>

Déjà MultiMedia Group LLC
Atlanta, GA

FROM OVERDRAFT TO OVERFLOW
3 Steps to Possession in a Recession

Copyright © 2010 by Déjà Multimedia Group LLC
All rights reserved.

Except as permitted under U.S. Copyright Act of 1976, no part of this publication may be reproduced, stored in a retrieval system, or transmitted in any form or by any means – electronic, mechanical, digital, photocopy, recording or any other – except for brief quotations in printed reviews, without the prior permission of the publisher.

All Scripture quotations, unless otherwise indicated, are taken from the King James Version (**KJV**) of the Bible.

Other Scripture quotations are from the following sources:

NLT: from the Holy Bible, New Living Translation, copyright © 1996, 2004, 2007. Used by permission of Tyndale House Publishers, Inc., Carol Stream, Illinois 60188. All rights reserved.

NIV: from the Holy Bible, New International Version®, NIV®. Copyright © 1973, 1978, 1984 by Biblica, Inc.™ Used by permission of Zondervan. All rights reserved worldwide.

AMP: from The Amplified Bible, Copyright © 1954, 1958, 1962, 1964, 1965, 1987 by The Lockman Foundation. Used by permission. www.Lockman.org

MSG: from The Message. Copyright © 1993, 1994, 1995, 1996, 2000, 2001, 2002. Used by permission of NavPress Publishing Group.

CEV: from the Contemporary English Version Copyright © 1991, 1992, 1995 by American Bible Society, Used by Permission.

Emphasis in scripture quotations has been added by the author.

Every effort has been made to give proper credit for all stories, poems, and quotations. If for any reason proper credit has not been given, please notify the author or publisher and proper notation will be given on future printing.

Published by Déjà MultiMedia Group LLC
www.DejaMultimedia.com

Joyner, Dawn.
   From Overdraft to Overflow: 3 Steps to Possession in a Recession
   *Spiritual Health * Personal Growth * Inspirational * Financial Management*

ISBN-10:   0-615-40555-X
ISBN-13:   978-0-615-40555-1

Printed in the United States of America

DECLARATION

*I thank God for entrusting me with such an
honorable assignment to share with His people
the potent power of this "Master Plan".
Right in the midst of my mess,
God made me a messenger of His message.*

*BE ENCOURAGED.
God is no respecter of persons.
No matter where you are, no matter what you've done
and no matter where you've been, if you are useable,
God can use you.*

**I AM who I am because GOD IS Who He is.
I DO what I do because GOD DID what He did.**

TABLE OF CONTENTS

THE MASTER DEBUT	11
Detrimental Dilemma	15
THE MASTER DESIGN	23
Step One: Master Your Mind	27
Deliberate Distractions	29
Destiny of Dominion	59
Divine Connection	86
Step Two: Master Your Mouth	105
Disturbing Dialect	107
Divine Ammunition	123
Divine Intervention	150
Step Three: Master Your Money	175
Deceptive Data Dispelled	177
Dynamic Duo	210
THE MASTER DECISION	235
Decide to Abide	239
Destination: Transformation	256
Divine Power Tool Box	265

DEDICATION

This book is dedicated with love to

MY HUSBAND
Christopher Robert Joyner, Sr.

&

MY FOUR SPECIAL GIFTS
Brian Larawn Robinson
Katrina Jeniece Copney-Robinson
Larry Tyrique Robinson
Christopher Robert Joyner, II

My Daughter from another Mother
ShaLishah Joy McCullough

DEFERENCE

*Individuals whose presence in my life
has made a profound impact on my life*

My Mother
Barbara L. Copney

My Gramma
Queen Esther Copney

My Favorite Cousin
Kenya M. Golds

My Sister from another Mother
Wanda D. Trotman

YOM & Matt
Virginia & Willie Madden

PHENOMENAL WOMAN MINISTRIES SUPREME TEAM
*Sonja P. Fulcher, Colleen Ortiz-Ferguson, Janet Allen,
Lisette Umpierre, Tyra Frazier-Atwood,
Carol Cooper, Dianne Hampton*

THE MASTER DEBUT

"From small beginnings come great things."
~ *Unknown* ~

Detrimental Dilemma

  We live in a society that is plagued with a severe case of instant gratification syndrome; a society where quick fixes are desired and encouraged.

  If you have picked up this book because you are looking for a "quick fix" – you should close this book, put it down and keep looking.

  You won't find one here.

  At first glance, the title may imply that this book offers some sort of "quick fix" to the miserable state of this current economy – to the miserable state of *your* current economy.

  It does not.

  If you have picked up this book because you are tired of living life by default and are ready to live life by God's divine design – an abundant life of power, peace and prosperity – you should sit back and relax, put your feet up and keep reading.

  The sole purpose of this book is to communicate to you that, even in the midst of this economic earthquake, there is still power in the Word of God to work wonders in our life *if* we learn how to work the Word of God into our life.

This book contains a practical three-step course of action that has the power to change what happens **NEXT** in your life – depending, of course, on *your* own personal course of action.

Although these three steps, which are strictly based on the powerful principles and promises found in the Word of God, have the ability to produce miraculous results in our life, they most certainly should not be considered to be some magical formula.

They are not.

Our Majestic God is not a magician and His Holy Word is not a book of magic.

However, Hebrews 4:12 assures us that the Word of God is alive and full of **P**owerful, **O**perative, **W**ise, **E**mpowering, **R**efreshing words that never change but have the power to change life.

STEP ONE: MASTER YOUR MIND

STEP TWO: MASTER YOUR MOUTH

STEP THREE: MASTER YOUR MONEY

I call this three-step course of action the "**Master Plan**"…

…and it is my belief that this Master Plan **IS** the **Master's Plan** for our new life *in Christ*.

Each individual element of this Master Plan, in and of itself, is prolific and profound, but integrated their impact is far more impressive.

Numerous books have been authored about each element of this Master Plan individually, but very few speak to the undeniable synergism of harmonizing all three.

In light of this current catastrophic economy, you may be tempted to skim through Step One: Master Your Mind, slip past Step Two: Master Your Mouth and skip to Step Three: Master Your Money.

If that is your choice, realize this:

- Money is not our true problem therefore money will not be our true solution.

- You will never be able to master your money if you don't first master your mind and your mouth.

You see, until we master our mind to *believe* God's precious promises of power, peace and prosperity for our life, we will never master our mouth to *speak* His precious promises of power, peace and prosperity for our life…over our life.

Until we master our mouth to *speak* God's precious promises of power, peace and prosperity for our life over our life, we will never *see* God's precious promises of power, peace and prosperity in our life.

While I suspect that the title of this book may incite controversy and condemnation, I expect that reading this book will ignite conversation and contemplation.

The terminology in the title of this book may give the impression that its content is related solely to finances.

It is not.

Yes, "overdraft" is a term generally related to being financially overdrawn and "overflow" is a fashionable buzzword in the body of Christ that has been adamantly shunned by some because of its direct association with what's been dubbed "the prosperity message". But overdraft *and* overflow extend beyond just the financial realm; they affect every area of our life.

For those of you who vehemently snub the prosperity message, my humble advice to you is this…have a little talk with Jesus; He preached the first prosperity message in John 10:10 (AMP)…

> **"I came that they may have and enjoy life, and have it in abundance (to the full, till it overflows)."**

What this book does address is the spiritual deficiency that has produced the pandemic overdraft and the spiritual efficiency required to produce the paramount overflow.

Every "believer" (that includes everyone because everyone believes something) is encouraged to read this book, but this Master Plan is specifically written to born-again believers who believe that God's Word has inherent power to transform lives because our lives have been transformed by that inherent power.

Even more precisely, this Master Plan will only work for a select group of born-again believers – *believers who believe God.*

My prayer for every born-again believer reading this book is that the God of our Lord Jesus Christ, the Father of glory, give you the spirit of wisdom and revelation so that you can get to know Him better. I also pray that your heart is enlightened so you fully understand the blessed hope God gave us when He chose us to be His own. I pray that you will be empowered as you discover just how rich and glorious an inheritance we have *in Christ* (Ephesians 1:17-18).

I admonish you to personalize and pray this anointed prayer before you continue reading this book. If, however, you choose to continue reading past this point without personalizing and praying this anointed prayer, you run the risk of reading this book through religious spectacles, the major source of speculation that has caused so much confusion and controversy in the body of Christ.

If you choose to continue reading past this point without permitting the Holy Spirit to dismantle and dispose of your religious spectacles and enable you to read this book with the eyes of faith, the information shared in this book will appear radical, the author fanatical, and your religious feathers will be ruffled leaving you outraged and offended...which is certainly not my intent.

If, however, you pray and personalize this anointed prayer with a receptive spirit, the Spirit of Truth will guide you into the absolute truth of God's Word. Then, like the blind man whose eyes Jesus opened in John 9:38, you will say, *"Lord, I believe"* and worship God for what He's done.

If you are a "nonbeliever" – someone who does not believe in God – and this book has come into your possession, realize that nothing happens by chance. My earnest prayer is that you will continue to read this book and as you read, that the Spirit of God will minister to your heart.

People of God, it *is* possible for us to live life by God's divine design in this life – on this earth…*if* we erase religious practices that have made the Word of God ineffective in our life and embrace relationship principles that make the Word of God operate in full effect in our life.

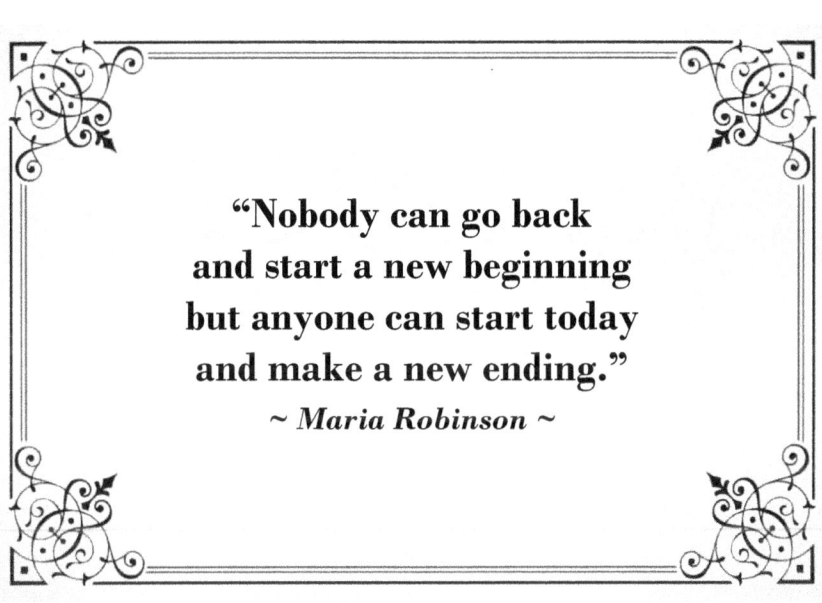

"Nobody can go back
and start a new beginning
but anyone can start today
and make a new ending."
~ *Maria Robinson* ~

THE MASTER DESIGN

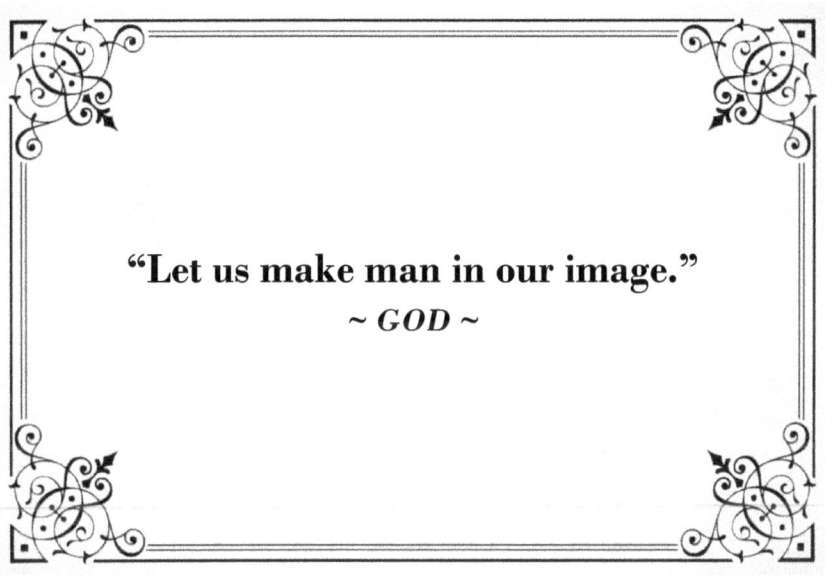

"Let us make man in our image."
~ *GOD* ~

STEP ONE:
MASTER YOUR MIND

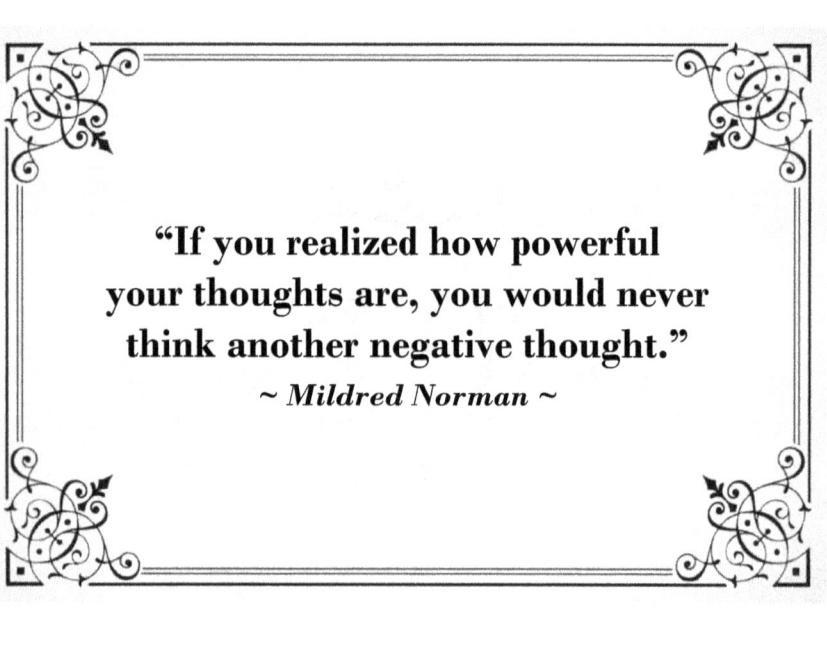

DELIBERATE DISTRACTIONS

IDENTITY THEFT, a disturbing trend that recently emerged in this country and quickly became the fastest growing crime in the United States over the past decade, has long been the fastest growing "crime" in the body of Christ.

Jesus warns us in John 10:10 that the thief's purpose is to steal, kill and destroy. Peter echoes Jesus' sentiments in 1 Peter 5:8 (NLT)…

> **"Stay alert! Watch out for your great enemy, the devil. He prowls around like a roaring lion, looking for someone to devour."**

Even with this sound counsel at our disposal, the chief thief has been quite successful at stealing identities, killing dreams and destroying relationships of the people of God.

Deliberate distractions are the root cause of identity theft. They are quite possibly *the* most powerful tools in Satan's war chest.

Shrewdly and strategically, he has incorporated a wide variety of deliberate distractions into our every day lives designed to deceive us about our true identity *in Christ* and discourage us about the prospect of receiving the promises of God…in this life.

Deliberate distractions are specifically and skillfully designed to divert our focus from the promises we've received in the Word and direct our focus to the problems we experience in this world.

Deliberate distractions invoke fear, inflame our feelings, inflict our finances, initiate strained relationships with our family and friends, instigate memories of our former life, infringe on our focus and ultimately, infect our faith.

The more we entertain deliberate distractions that stem from fear, our feelings, our finances, our family, our friends or our former life, the more they interfere with our focus on our faith.

We have clearly underestimated our adversary, that old serpent called the Devil and Satan. He is extremely passionate about fulfilling his purpose. Daily, he deliberately distracts us with the business or should I say "busyness" of life because he knows that the longer he keeps us distracted, the more likely we are to stay distracted and the more distracted we stay, the easier it becomes for him to swoop in and swallow us whole.

He's always up on his game because the clock is ticking and he's running out of time. He's never slack because he doesn't have the luxury to slip up but he uses deliberate distractions to see to it that *we* are slack so that *we* slip up.

He knows his destiny has been sealed. He knows our destiny has been sealed. His end game is to "unseal" our destiny of dominion *in Christ* and seal a destiny of destruction with him.

Unlike most believers, he is consistent and persistent about fulfilling his purpose. He understands that consistency and persistency are the secret to success…his and ours. His success is contingent on his knowledge that 1) the only thing most believers are consistent about is being inconsistent and 2) most believers are passive about persistence.

For believers, being consistent means we stand firm – unshakable and unmovable – on God's Word despite the strong negative current of the world swirling fiercely around us attempting to consume us.

Being persistent means we persevere with unwavering tenacity and push through with uncompromising fortitude in spite of the deceptive and discouraging deliberate distractions Satan sends our way.

Consistency and persistency are two major challenges in the life of every believer that *must* be conquered if we plan to live life by God's divine design.

On the flip side of the coin, we have clearly overestimated our adversary, that old serpent called the Devil and Satan. Peter clearly tells us that Satan prowls around *like* a roaring lion looking for someone to devour but we treat him as if *he is* a roaring lion. And even if he was the king of the beasts, the King of all kings has given us **ALL** power over him.

> "Behold, *I give unto you power* to tread on serpents and scorpions, and *over all the power of the enemy*: and nothing shall by any means hurt you."
>
> **Luke 10:19**

Let the people of God say…

"I'VE GOT THE POWER!"

Yes, people of God, we've got the power but we cower in his presence because he has successfully deceived us about our true identity *in Christ*.

Satan has a Master's Degree in the Art of Deception. In fact, he *is* the master of deception. His entire kingdom is established and exists on a firm foundation of deception.

Identity theft is his primary M.O. – his modus operandi – because *he knows* who we really are *in Christ*. He works diligently to keep us deliberately distracted because he also knows that once *we* find out and start acting like *we know* who we are *in Christ*…it's a wrap.

Now you may not think that *you* are the victim of identity theft but…

- If you have resigned yourself to living life by default – accepting life "as is" until we all get to heaven…then yes, *you* are the victim of identity theft.

- If you, along with the rest of the world, find yourself getting distressed and depressed as you assess this mess…then yes, *you* are the victim of identity theft.

- If the pressure of looking at your overdrawn bank account elevates your pressure because it always seems like there's more month at the end of the money…then yes, *you* are the victim of identity theft.

- If you are drowning in a sea of debt – stretching dollars and pinching pennies trying to make ends meet…then yes, *you* are the victim of identity theft.

- If you are developing and allowing stress-related illnesses to take permanent residence in your body, accepting it as "the will of God" …then yes, *you* are the victim of identity theft.

- If you are beginning to question your faith in the faithfulness of our faithful Father…then yes, *you* are the victim of identity theft.

If any *one* of the above holds true for you, then you, my friend, are the victim of identity theft.

Before we move forward to identify the elixir for this epidemic of identity theft in the body of Christ, let's take a glimpse backward and briefly examine three key cases of identity theft that occurred in the Word.

Identity theft originated in heaven. And what's interesting is that the originator of identity theft was the original victim of identity theft.

Lucifer deceived himself about his own true identity. He deceived himself to believe that he, the creature, was greater in stature and splendor than God, the Creator.

Boldly he defied God, declared his position and deceived one-third of the angels to willingly turn their backs on God and give up all they had...for what he had to offer. Ultimately, this rebellion resulted in the very first exodus – expulsion from heaven.

Jesus says in Luke 10:18 (CEV)...

"I saw Satan fall from heaven like a flash of lightning."

The rebellion in heaven was centered around Lucifer's perverted burning desire to be "like God". Since that didn't work out so well for him he decided to go after the next best thing – the people who were "like God". To this day, Satan is still going after the people who are "like God".

Adam and Eve were an express replica of God. They were "like God". What's amazing is the basis of the deception in the Garden of Eden was they would be "like God" if they ate of the fruit of the tree of knowledge of good and evil.

Eve became the victim of identity theft when she allowed Satan to deceive her to believe that she could become...somebody *she already was* (Genesis 3:5).

Can you see just how easy it is for Satan to deceive us when we don't know who we really are?

Eve then deceived herself to believe that maybe she *was* missing out on something better than what she already had. Like the fallen angels, Eve gave up everything *she already had*…for what Satan had to offer. As a result, the second exodus occurred – expulsion from the garden of God.

> **"So he drove out the man; and he placed at the east of the garden of Eden Cherubims, and a flaming sword which turned every way, to keep the way of the tree of life."**
>
> **Genesis 3:24**

The third case of identity theft, which has the closest resemblance to the epidemic of identity theft in the body of Christ occurred in the wilderness.

With great power and a mighty hand, God delivered the children of Israel from Egypt, the land of bondage. As they journeyed through the wilderness on their way to the Promised Land, He guided their path as a pillar of cloud by day and a pillar of fire by night.

With great care and a loving hand, He fed them miraculously with manna from heaven daily and quenched their thirst with an abundance of water from a rock. They were mighty in battle because the hand of the Lord was with them.

God made provision for His children to live comfortably during their wilderness experience on the way to their Promised Land. Yet, after all the wondrous works of God's hands, they became victims of identity theft.

God instructed Moses to send twelve men – a man from every tribe – to check out the land God had *already* given the children of Israel. After surveying the land for forty days, ten of the twelve returned to the congregation of Israel with a message of confirmation and apprehension.

Out of one side of their mouth, they spoke a word of confirmation about God's promise concerning the land of Canaan…

> "We entered the land you sent us to explore, and it is indeed a bountiful country – a land flowing with milk and honey. Here is the kind of fruit it produces."
>
> Numbers 13:27 NLT

Out of the other side of their mouth, they spoke a word of apprehension...

> "But the people living there are powerful, and their towns are large and fortified. We even saw giants there...We can't go up against them! They are stronger than we are!"
>
> Numbers 13:28, 31 NLT

These ten men became victims of identity theft because they were deliberately distracted by the giants in the land as opposed to being inspired and intent on receiving God's promise of possession to them.

The subtlety of deception is that the deceived is usually unaware that they are being deceived...either by oneself or someone else. Lucifer deceived himself and then deceived one-third of the angels. Eve was deceived by the sneaky snake and then deceived herself.

The ten spies were deceived by what they *perceived* to be a problem amid the promises. The seeds of deception that they in turn planted in the minds of the congregation of Israel blossomed into weeds of destruction that strangled what little faith they had in God.

The delivery of this mixed message afflicted the congregation of Israel with analysis paralysis. Instead of blessing God for His promise, they began analyzing the pseudo-problems in the land of Canaan and became paralyzed by the word of these ten fearful men.

This journey through the wilderness was never meant to be a final destination for the children of Israel. It was only meant to be a passageway from the land of bondage to the land of Promise.

Instead of reflecting on their extraordinary exodus from where they came from and praising God for where He promised they were going, the children of Israel constantly complained about the deliberate distractions in the wilderness and protested against God about where they were.

It was more than God could take…

> **"…not one of these people will ever enter that land. They have all seen My glorious presence and the miraculous signs I performed both in Egypt and in the wilderness, but again and again they have tested Me by refusing to listen to my voice. They will never even see the land I swore to give their ancestors.** *None of those who have treated Me with contempt will ever see it…* **They will be destroyed here in this wilderness, and here they will die!"**
>
> Numbers 14:22-23, 35 NLT

God's purpose for this journey through the wilderness was to humble the children of Israel and evaluate their performance. He wanted to see if they would trust Him implicitly and obey Him immediately (Deuteronomy 8:2).

Instead of being humbled by this wilderness experience, the children of Israel repeatedly humiliated God by not trusting His Word or obeying His voice.

They became victims of identity theft because they allowed the deception of who they were in their *own* eyes and who they thought they were in the eyes of the giants to overrule who they were in the eyes of God. They allowed the deliberate distractions in the wilderness to press them into an unhealthy desire to *go back* to the land of bondage.

> **"Wouldn't it be better for us to go back to Egypt?"**
>
> Numbers 14:3 NIV

> *What made them think "back" was better?*

Do you ever feel like "going back" when the pressure presses in? Do you mumble and grumble about your problems when you should be meditating and confessing the promises of God?

Not long ago, the Holy Spirit reminded me of this particular story as I mumbled and grumbled about "going back". As I meditated on this story, it was humbling for me to realize that at the very least, my mumbling and grumbling might extend my stay in the wilderness longer than I wanted or needed to be there.

The children of Israel spent forty *years* on a trip that should have taken eleven *days* to complete.

If you stop to think about it, maybe you are experiencing an extended stay in the "wilderness" because all you do is mumble and grumble about where you are.

My worst nightmare was that my mumbling and grumbling might completely prevent me from entering my land of Promise.

We may not realize it but in God's eyes, all our mumbling and grumbling boils down to unbelief. Unbelief provokes God because it is a grievous sign of contempt.

In a court of law "contempt of court" is willful disobedience of or open disrespect for the rules and orders of the court. If one is found "in contempt" the judge will impose sanctions.

The origin of this modern day practice can clearly be traced back to the Word of God. For their provocation and acts of contempt toward Him, we find God imposing sanctions on the children of Israel in Numbers 14:26-35 and in the end…

> **"…we see that they were not able to enter [into His rest], because of their unwillingness to adhere to and trust in and rely on God *[unbelief had shut them out]*."**
>
> **Hebrews 3:19 AMP**

Unbelief even shut God's prophet, Moses, out from entering into the Promised Land. In recounting the circumstances surrounding their rebellion, Moses tells the children of Israel *"And the Lord was also angry with me because of you. He said to me, 'Moses, not even you will enter the Promised Land'"* (Deuteronomy 1:37 NLT). But what the Lord actually said to Moses and Aaron in Numbers 20:12 (CEV) was...

> **"Because <u>*you*</u> *refused to believe* in my power, these people did not respect me. And so, you will not be the ones to lead them into the land I have promised."**

The inception of deception, which eventually translates to unbelief, comes from listening to the wrong storyteller tell the wrong story.

One-third of the heavenly host listened to Lucifer's fabulous fable of his lavish leadership. Eve listened to a talking serpent's story about the bountiful benefit of feasting on the fruit from the tree of knowledge of good and evil. The children of Israel listened to the exaggerated exposé of ten spies about their exploration of the Promised Land.

The common thread weaved through the fabric of Satan's deceptive tactics, in each instance, was his astounding ability to convince the listener that what he had to give was much better than what they had already been given.

Satan's deceptions are successful because his distractions have appeal.

THAT WAS THEN...THIS IS NOW

"The thing that has been – it is what will be again...and *there is nothing new under the sun.*"

Ecclesiastes 1:9 AMP

The parallel between the experiences of God's chosen people, the children of Israel and God's redeemed people, the body of Christ, is one of monumental significance.

With great power and a mighty hand, God, *in Christ*, delivered us from the kingdom of darkness, where we were entangled in the bondage of sin (Colossians 1:13). As we journey through this life, God's Word is a lamp to light our path (Psalm 119:105).

With great care and a loving hand, God supplies everything we need from His glorious and infinite riches *in Christ* (Philippians 4:19).

Everything we need to live a life that pleases the Father has been made available to us *in Christ* (2 Peter 1:3). We are mighty in battle because God always causes us to triumph *in Christ* (2 Corinthians 2:14).

We can fight the good fight of faith because He has provided us with a divine arsenal of lethal weapons that enables us to demolish every evil weapon that the enemy forms against us and dodge every evil snare that the enemy sets for us (2 Corinthians 10:4).

God, *in Christ*, has made provision for us to live comfortably during our "wilderness experience" on the way to our Promised Land. Yet, after all the wondrous works of God's hands, we have become victims of identity theft.

Out of one side of our mouth, we praise God for Who He is and for doing what He's done in our life but no sooner than things get tricky and the situation gets sticky, we curse God out of the other side of our mouth for *"letting all these things happen to us"*.

"Out of the same mouth come praise and cursing. My brothers, this should not be."

James 3:10 NIV

This journey through the wilderness was never meant to be a final destination for the body of Christ. It was only meant to be a passageway from the land of bondage to the land of Promise – a life lived by God's divine design right here on this earth.

Instead of reflecting on our remarkable redemption from the kingdom of darkness and praising God for His promises, we constantly complain about all the deliberate distractions in the wilderness and protest against God about where we are.

> **"Because of the LORD's great love we are not consumed, for his compassions never fail. They are new every morning; great is your faithfulness."**
>
> **Lamentations 3:22-23 NIV**

God's purpose for this journey through the wilderness is to humble us under His mighty hand and evaluate our performance; to see if we will trust Him implicitly and obey Him immediately.

Instead of being humbled by this wilderness experience, we repeatedly humiliate God by not trusting His Word or obeying His voice.

We have become victims of identity theft because we have allowed the deception of who we are in our *own* eyes and who we think we are in the eyes of others to overrule who we are in the eyes of God – who God says we are *in Christ*, what we can do *through Christ*, and where we can go *with Christ*.

We allow deliberate distractions in our wilderness experience to press us into an unhealthy desire to go back to the land of bondage – our "comfort zone".

What makes us think back is better? Why are we more comfortable in bondage?

Unfortunately, this unhealthy desire has become an unpleasant reality for many believers.

With the exception of Joshua and Caleb, identity theft cost the entire congregation of Israel, from the age of twenty and up, their promised inheritance.

Joshua and Caleb were the two of the twelve that demonstrated a different spirit than the other ten men. They trusted God implicitly and were ready to obey Him immediately.

In the midst of the madness, Caleb stepped up to the plate and...

> "...stilled the people before Moses, and said, Let us go up at once, and possess it; *for we are well able to overcome it.*"
>
> **Numbers 13:30**

Joshua and Caleb demonstrated a spirit of faith...

> "It is written: 'I believed; therefore I have spoken.' With that same *spirit of faith* we also believe and therefore speak."
>
> **2 Corinthians 4:13 NIV**

Joshua and Caleb had a press in their spirit because the portrait of their extraordinary exodus from Egypt was freshly painted on the canvas of their minds. They spoke with authority and audacity because they believed God. They believed they possessed the power to possess God's promise. Their confidence was extreme because they were extremely confident in the Power behind that power.

Are there any Joshua and Caleb's in the body of Christ today? Is there anyone who, with that same spirit of faith, will believe God and speak His promises over their life with authority and audacity?

You know, following the crowd is not always such a good thing...

> "...For wide is the gate and broad is the road that leads to destruction, and many enter through it."
>
> **Matthew 7:13 NIV**

People of God, if we don't want to miss out on our promised inheritance here on this earth, in the midst of the madness, we need to step up to the plate...so we can step into the promises.

It's high time for us to stop being deceived and discouraged by deliberate distractions that try to press us into going back or paralyze us into standing still when we should be still standing on God's Word and pressing on to our Promised Land.

It's high time for us to press into our walk with authority *and* audacity. We *already* have the authority to pull rank on the devil but we lack the audacity to invoke our authority to pull rank on the devil.

It's high time for us to...

Praise God for what He's already done in our life

Receive what He's already done in our life in our spirit

Expect what He's already done to manifest in our life

See what He's already done through the eye of faith *so we can*

See what He's already done in our life...in our life!

Now more than ever, we need this **PRESS** in our spirit so we can:

- **PRESS** through the pressure
- **PRESS** past this mess
- **PRESS** into the promises and
- **PRESS** toward the mark!

It's high time for us to firmly position ourselves in the presence of our Perfect Holy Father to protect us from pondering on the pretense that His promises have not prevailed and will not produce in our life.

> *We Possess the Power
> to Possess the Promises!*

PAUSE and let this statement marinate in your mind until it saturates your spirit.

Now personalize it and say...

"I POSSESS THE POWER TO POSSESS THE PROMISES!"

These eight words are the rock-solid foundation on which Step One: Master Your Mind is built.

2 Corinthians 1:20 (NLT) tells us that *"**ALL** of God's promises have been fulfilled in Christ with a resounding 'Yes!'"* But before we can master our mind to receive God's promises, we must master our mind to believe that:

- **YES!** ALL of God's promises belong to us...*already*!
- **YES!** It is up to *us* to take possession of God's promises!
- **YES!** WE possess the power to possess the promises!

Although God conferred upon Joshua and Caleb their promised inheritance that day in the wilderness, the promise was made manifest forty-five years later and forty-five years later, Caleb still had a press in his spirit...(Joshua 14:10-12 NLT)

> "...**Today I am eighty-five years old.** *I am as strong now* **as I was when Moses sent me on that journey, and I can still travel and fight as well as I could then. So give me the hill country** *that the LORD promised me.* **You will remember that as scouts we found the descendants of Anak living there in great, walled towns. But if the LORD is with me,** *I will drive them out of the land, just as the LORD said.*"

Joshua and Caleb received their promised inheritance because they refused to be deceived by the deliberate distractions. Instead, they chose to firmly fix their hearts on what God had promised. Because of their implicit trust in and immediate obedience to God, they were immune to the ensuing identity crisis that occurred that day in the wilderness as a result of identity theft.

Identity theft has also created a major identity crisis in the body of Christ. This identity crisis has far too many believers living life by default when our true calling is to live life by God's divine design.

It was never our Heavenly Father's intention that we live life by default...accepting whatever happens and whatever comes our way as "the will of God", living from paycheck to paycheck, trying to make ends meet.

It was always our Heavenly Father's intention that we live life by His divine design...accepting what's *already* happened and what's *already* come our way *in Christ* as His perfect will, living from faith to faith and realizing that, *in Christ*, the ends have met.

Now don't get it twisted, not every believer is suffering from identity crisis. There are many believers who know who they really are *in Christ* and do believe in their heart that God's promises are true to them and are living life by God's divine design.

Based on my personal observation, I suspect that the vast majority of believers *do not* know who they really are *in Christ*, *do not* believe in their heart that God's promises are true to them and basically, *are not* living life by God's divine design.

This allegation may appear judgmental and pretentious but my statement is based on Jesus' assertion in Matthew 12:34 (NLT)...

> **"For whatever is in your heart determines what you say."**

Our casual conversation is a reflection of our cardiac condition. In other words, whatever is in our heart will eventually come out of our mouth.

There is one expression, in particular, that frequently comes up in casual conversation among believers that confirms my suspicion that quite a few believers are experiencing an identity crisis as a result of identity theft.

Somebody lit the match and this cliché has spread like wildfire in the body of Christ. From the pulpit to the door, from the balcony to the floor, the people of God are confidently uttering what they deem to be a "confession of faith".

It is not.

> *"God Is Getting Ready To..."*

It's really a "confession of fallacy" – a counterfeit confession…

"God is getting ready to turn my situation around"

"God is getting ready to heal my body"

"God is getting ready to restore my marriage"

"God is getting ready to bring my unruly child home"

"God is getting ready to bless me with a new job"

"God is getting ready to increase my finances"

"God is getting ready to get me out of debt"

"God is getting ready to bless me with a fine home"

"God is getting ready to bless me with a new car"

"God is getting ready to do everything He promised me He'd do"

I promise you, that if you listen closely during the course of a casual conversation between the saints or during the course of an emotionally-charged sermon or even at the jumpstart of a praise break, you will hear somebody sharing what *God is getting ready to* do.

IDENTITY THEFT!

My question is profound…Why are so many believers waiting for God to do something that He has *already* done?

My answer is simple…

Identity theft has created an identity crisis that has inhibited our ability to believe that God's promises *already* belong to us and therefore impeded our ability to receive the promises of God.

God has *already* done everything He's going to do for us *in Christ*.

> **"But all things are from God, Who *through Jesus Christ reconciled us to Himself* [received us into favor, brought us into harmony with Himself]…"**
>
> **2 Corinthians 5:18 AMP**

God has *already* said everything He's going to say about who we are *in Christ*.

> **"Therefore, if anyone is *in Christ, he is a new creation*; the old has gone, the new has come!"**
>
> **2 Corinthians 5:17 NIV**

God has *already* given us everything we need *in Christ* to live a life that pleases Him.

> **"By his divine power, God *has given us everything we need* for living a godly life."**
>
> 2 Peter 1:3 NLT

God has *already* given us everything we need to produce wealth.

> **"But remember the LORD your God, *for it is he who gives you the ability to produce wealth*, and so confirms his covenant, which he swore to your forefathers, as it is today."**
>
> Deuteronomy 8:18 NIV

God has *already* given us everything we need to stop the enemy right in his tracks.

> **"Behold! *I have given you authority and power* to trample upon serpents and scorpions, and [physical and mental strength and ability] *over all the power that the enemy [possesses]*; and nothing shall in any way harm you."**
>
> Luke 10:19 AMP

Let the people of God say...

"I'VE GOT EVERYTHING I NEED TO DO EVERYTHING I NEED TO DO!"

Listen, this is not something new. We have been in possession of this power for quite some time. But because we have not invested quality time immersed in the Word so we can master our mind to this absolute truth, we've become victims of identity theft and have been living powerless lives in crisis when our true calling is to live powerful lives *in Christ*.

This catchy cliché is a deception that has so many believers prayerfully and patiently sitting in the "waiting room" waiting for what *God is getting ready to* do.

Your question may be *"Well, doesn't God want us to wait on Him?"*

Absolutely! The Psalmist clearly admonishes us to...

> **"Wait on the LORD: be of good courage, and he shall strengthen thine heart: wait, I say, on the LORD."**
> Psalm 27:14

> **"Wait on the LORD, and keep his way, and he shall exalt thee to inherit the land."**
> Psalm 37:34

However, based on my modest knowledge of his relationship with God, it is my belief that what David is charging us to do in these two passages of scripture is "wait on" the Lord – to *"call upon, minister to or serve"* the Lord – not simply "wait" on the Lord.

I believe what has happened is many believers are sitting in the waiting room waiting *for* the Lord. They have chosen to *"remain inactive in one place while expecting"* God to do whatever it is they think He's *getting ready to* do. In the meantime, this dormant lifestyle has resulted in a life of crisis because the Word clearly tells us...

> **"A little extra sleep, a little more slumber, a little folding of the hands to rest – then poverty will pounce on you like a bandit; scarcity will attack you like an armed robber."**
> Proverbs 24:33-34 NLT

It's only when we spend quality time immersed in God's presence that our courage is charged, our heart is strengthened and we experience fullness of joy and times of refreshing. It's only when we spend quality time seeking His way of doing and being right, that we will inherit God's promises.

Before we can wait *for* the Lord, we must wait *on* the Lord. David waited patiently *for* the LORD (Psalm 40:1) because he first spent quality time waiting *on* the Lord (Psalm 25:21).

If we don't spend quality time waiting *on* the Lord, time spent in the waiting room waiting *for* the Lord will certainly be a faith-depleting experience.

It's only *after* we *"call upon, minister to or serve"* the Lord that we can *"stay in one place"* with patience and composure *"in anticipation"* of what God has *already* done for us to manifest in our life in due season.

> **"The eyes of all wait for You [looking, watching, and expecting] and You give them their food in due season."**
>
> **Psalm 145:15 AMP**

As we wait on and for the Lord, we have this blessed assurance...

> **"...let none that *wait on* thee be ashamed."**
>
> **Psalm 25:3**

> **"I am the LORD: for they shall not be ashamed that *wait for* me."**
>
> **Isaiah 49:23**

What's interesting is God is also sitting in the "waiting room". He's *waiting for* us to lay aside every weight and *wait on* Him so He can *wait on* us.

He *"remains in expectation"* for us to surrender our stress and strife and *"call upon or minister to"* Him so He can *"minister to and serve us"* with His choice blessings *in Christ*.

All this time, believers have been sitting in the waiting room waiting for God to do something "special" in our life and all this time, God has been sitting in the waiting room waiting for us to do something "special" *with* our life...with what He's *already* done for us.

If you wanna get down to the nitty-gritty, what many believers have *really* been doing in the "waiting room" is waiting for God to do or say or give us...*something else*.

This catchy cliché – *"God is getting ready to"* – is a flagrant contradiction of God's Word that has been craftily concocted by Satan to deliberately distract us from what God has *already* done.

From the very beginning, Satan's strategy has been to talk us out of what's already ours. Well, what he's really done is gotten *us* to talk ourselves out of what's already ours.

This catchy cliché transfers the authority delegated to us by God back to God. God had His part to do…we have our part to do. God has already done *His* part. He has already done what *we think* He's *getting ready to* do. He has already said what *we* need to do to receive what He's already done. He's just been waiting for us *to do* what He's already said so we can receive what He's already given to us.

If we don't master our mind to the absolute truth that we are already in possession of the power to possess God's promises and then put the pedal to the metal and possess God's promises, we will just continue to sit prayerfully and patiently in the waiting room waiting for God to do or say or give us…*something else.*

Hypothetically speaking, what makes us think that we would even do "something else" when we haven't even done what God has *already* said we should do?

Listen, God cannot change what He's already done and He will not change what He's already said about how we receive what He's already given us (Malachi 3:6; Hebrews 13:8).

God said exactly what He meant and He meant exactly what He said.

> **"My covenant will I not break, nor alter the thing that is gone out of my lips."**
> **Psalm 89:34**

Our part is to alter our crisis-filled lifestyle by aligning it with what He's already said in His Word so we can receive what He's already given us and live a Christ-centered lifestyle.

Our part is to abolish identity theft, abandon life by default, assume our rightful position *in Christ* and accept God's plan for us to live life by divine design – an abundant life of power, peace and prosperity.

Let the people of God say...

"I'VE GOT TO DO MY PART!"

If we want to change what we are seeing in our lives, we have to change what we "seeing" in our lives. We have to shift our focus from what we are seeing to what we *want* to see in our lives – all that God has already given us.

If we continue to focus on what we're seeing – all the problems we're having and all the pain we're feeling – we'll continue to see more problems and feel more pain.

- We have to shift our focus from the deliberate distractions we see in the world to the *precious promises* we see in the Word.

- We have to shift our focus from identity theft to *identity truth.*

- We have to shift our focus from identity crisis to our *true identity in Christ.*

- We have to shift our focus from what's going on outside of us to *what's going on inside* of us.

You see, the degree to which we prosper externally (physically, financially or otherwise) is directly proportional to the degree to which we prosper internally (spiritually).

> "Beloved, I pray that you may *prosper in every way* and [that your body] may keep well, even as [I know] your *soul keeps well and prospers.*"
>
> 3 John 2 AMP

Let the people of God say…

"That's God Divine Order."

Unfortunately, many believers are walking around with an **"OUT OF ORDER"** sign blinking overhead because identity theft has shifted our focus from internal prosperity to external prosperity.

Our Creator created us to live from the inside out. And actually, we have been living from the inside out. But because we've digested more things of the world than the things of God, our internal reality remains more natural than supernatural and our external reality is a reflection of the same.

Each year, billions of dollars are spent to improve external appearances. Over $52 billion is spent annually in the weight loss and cosmetic surgery industries alone. At the end of the day, with all the magic pills and potions, creams and lotions, nips and tucks, there still exists an inexplicable internal void that people are constantly struggling to fill.

As spiritual beings, our spiritual health, the core of our existence, is our true life support system. Our physical body – whatever shape or size it may be – is an elaborate "earth suit", if you will, that houses our spirit and grants us legal access to occupy this physical realm as human beings.

King Solomon affirms the importance of monitoring our cardiac condition…

> "Guard your heart *above all else*, for it determines the course of your life."
>
> **Proverbs 4:23 NLT**

When discussing matters of the heart in God's Word, it is our recreated newborn spirits – our "Inside Man" – rather than the physical organ that is the subject matter. We are all well aware of the dangers of neglecting the condition of our physical heart, why should we be less concerned with the condition of our spiritual heart…especially since it determines the course of our life?

Realize this…as long as there is a disconnect in our spiritual health – as long as our spirits are not *securely* connected to God's Spirit, our life experience will always suffer to some degree.

Regardless of how much weight we lose, how much muscle we tone, how much face we lift, how much fat we nip or tummy we tuck, if our spirits are not *securely* connected to God's Spirit, we might look fabulously flawless on the outside, but on the inside, we will be fatally flawed.

Quite frankly, the main reason our physical health is impaired is because our spiritual health is inadequate.

Paul warns us in Romans 12:2 not to copy the culture and conduct of this world. Have we heeded his warning? Not at all. We've completely ignored it and have become so well-adjusted to the culture and conduct of this world that we fit right into it – as snug as a bug in a rug – without giving it a second thought.

We've let our guard down and allowed identity theft to creep in and induce an identity crisis that has us "Struggling To Resolve Everyday Situations Single-handedly"…which in due course results in STRESS.

Stress is the root cause of many physical disorders in our society. Results of scientific studies validate that there is a definite connection between stress and heart disease, diabetes, rheumatoid arthritis, cancer, asthma, obesity, migraine headaches, muscle tension, ulcers, anxiety, insomnia, hypertension, depression and a host of other physical disorders.

Stress has been defined in many different ways by many different sources but the definition on eHealthmd.com dovetails nicely with my point.

> *"Stress is the emotional and physical strain caused by our response to pressure from the outside world."*

In today's society, stress levels elevate because people become overwhelmed by the challenges they face and the obstacles they stumble upon in their daily life experience.

Stress levels elevate in the body of Christ because believers allow these outside challenges and obstacles to influence the Inside Man.

In His parable of the Sower in Mark 4, Jesus gives four scenarios of what happens when the seed – the Word of God – is sown. In the third scenario (4:19 AMP), He talks about the outcome of seed that is sown among thorns...

"Then the cares and anxieties of the world and distractions of the age, and the pleasure and delight and false glamour and deceitfulness of riches, and the craving and passionate desire for other things *creep in and choke and suffocate the Word, and it becomes fruitless.*"

Identity theft suppresses our craving for the things of God and heightens our worldly cravings. The more we seek to satisfy these worldly cravings the more we realize they are not as satisfying as we'd hoped they would be.

These unnatural cravings shift our focus from our covenant rights in the Word to the cares and anxieties of this world until what's going on around us surrounds and smothers us when what's going on inside us should drive and defend us.

As the stress escalates, we turn to medical professionals who customarily will offer solutions about how to better "manage" or "minimize" stress. Society believes that stress is a fact of nature.

I beg to differ. My Word tells me that *"God saw every thing that He had made, and, behold, it was very good"* (Genesis 1:31).

Let the people of God say...

"STRESS IS NOT OF GOD!"

James 1:17 (NLT) tells me that *"Whatever is good and perfect comes down to us from God our Father."* Stress is not good nor is it perfect.

Stress emerged after sin was established. Adam and Eve got stressed out when they realized they were naked. They were naked because Eve got stressed out when she "realized" that she was missing out on something more. Adam got even more stressed when he realized what he had allowed to happen...then blamed Eve.

We should not readily accept stress as a fact of nature because the fact of the matter is Jesus gave us the peace of God.

> **"Peace I leave with you; My [own] peace I now give and bequeath to you. Not as the world gives do I give to you.** *Do not let your hearts be troubled,* **neither let them be afraid. [Stop allowing yourselves to be agitated and disturbed; and do not permit yourselves to be fearful and intimidated and cowardly and unsettled.]"**
>
> **John 14:27 AMP**

God's peace is beyond human comprehension. God's peace keeps your Inside Man cool calm and collected in the midst of the storm.

Medical professionals are trained to conduct extensive evaluations to diagnose the problem and prescribe a treatment that, on occasion involves ingesting an assortment of chemical compositions aka "medicine" to deal with the psychological aspects of stress and/or the physiological defects that have resulted from stress.

Each year with the emergence of side effects and ineffective treatments, these medical professionals continue to offer "new and improved" products that boast "bigger and better" results.

But King Solomon, in Proverbs 4:20-22 (NLT) offers the wisest of treatments...

> "**My child,** *pay attention to what I say. Listen carefully to my words.* **Don't lose sight of them. Let them penetrate deep into your heart,** *for they bring life* **to those who find them, and** *healing to their whole body.*"

Modern medical science may provide temporary and rapid remedial solutions for specific ailments in our life but the Word of God provides permanent restoration and refinement for every area of our life.

It is obvious that the behavior and customs of this world are contrary to the behavior and customs of the Word. The only way you can quash the identity crisis is to come to the knowledge of our true identity *in Christ* by letting...

> "**...God transform you into a new person by changing the way you think.**"
>
> **Romans 12: 2 NLT**

The Prophet Isaiah tells us that *if* we fix our thoughts on the things of God and totally trust and have complete confidence in Him, we will experience an incomprehensible peace that will *guard our hearts and our minds in Christ Jesus* and subdue the pressures that may arise from the storms of life (Isaiah 26:3, Philippians 4:7).

If we would pay attention and listen carefully to what God tells us in His Word and allow His Word to penetrate the alcoves of our heart, when the pressures of life begin to press in and our minds begin to spin, we would immediately capture every rebellious thought and teach them to be obedient to Christ (2 Corinthians 10:5 NLT).

If we would spend more quality time strengthening our spiritual health, we will begin to exercise our right to *command* our body, our mind, our emotions, our family and financial issues and whatever else is out of line in our lives to align with the Word of God.

> **"You gave them authority over all things."** Now when it says "all things," it means *nothing is left out."*
>
> **Hebrews 2:8 NLT**

We have authority over every sickness and disease that attacks our body. We have authority over every toxic thought that attacks our mind. We have authority to take control of our erratic emotions.

We have authority over matters that threaten to destroy our family. We have authority over the financial challenges that threaten our sanity.

Let the people of God say…

"I'VE GOT THE POWER!"

In recent years, a popular question has been posed in the body of Christ…

"What Would Jesus Do"?

I preface that question with this question…

"What Would Jesus Think"?

Isn't that the natural order of things – to *think* before we *do*? (Well, at least that should be the natural order of things.)

When Satan tried to deliberately distract Jesus in the wilderness, Jesus was not even moved. There was *no way* Jesus could "do" what Satan wanted Him to do because there was *no way* Jesus could even "think" along those lines. His thoughts were aligned with God's thoughts.

Jesus couldn't identify with identity theft or experience an identity crisis because He had a sound mind. Jesus' mind was sound because His heart was divinely connected to His Father.

He was confident in Who He was…

- *in His humanity* – the Son of Man
- *in His divinity* – the Son of God

…and in His ability to do what He came to do.

For Jesus to successfully accomplish His assignment, it was vital that He remained divinely connected to His Father so He could maintain a calm and well-balanced mind.

If we are to successfully accomplish our assignment, we too, must remain divinely connected to our Father so we can maintain a calm and well-balanced mind.

Identity theft has spawned an identity crisis that has left many believers distressed, in debt and discontented.

While this epidemic is formidable and fateful, Jesus gives us an elixir for this epidemic of identity theft that is forceful and faithful…

> **"If you abide in My Word [hold fast to My teachings and *live in accordance with them*, you are truly my disciples. And you will know the Truth, and *the Truth shall make you free.*"**
>
> **John 8:31-32 AMP**

As we master our mind to believe the absolute truth of God's Word that our destiny is not one of destruction, we will be delivered from the deception of deliberate distractions, identity theft will dissipate, the identity crisis will disappear and we will walk boldly in our destiny of dominion as heirs of God and joint-heirs with Christ!

DESTINY OF DOMINION

God created us to live productive, profitable and prosperous lives; to cultivate and conserve the wondrous works of His hands *and* to exercise control and assume absolute authority over **ALL** the earth.

> *God created us to have DOMINION...*
> *not to be dominated.*

That was the divine design God had in mind when He created mankind.

After creating the fish of the sea, the fowl of the air, beast of the field, the cattle of the meadows, and every thing that creeps on this earth, God said *about* man in Genesis 1:26...

"Let us make man in our image, after our likeness."

In other words, God was saying "Let Us make man...like Us. Let the nature and appearance of this creature be a reflection of Our nature and Our appearance."

In today's terminology what that means is we have the DNA – **D**ivine **N**ature and **A**ppearance – of God. That means the Greatest Power resides inside of us. 1 John 4:4 (NLT) confirms it...

"...the Spirit who lives in you is greater than the spirit who lives in the world."

Let the people of God say...

"I'VE GOT THE POWER!"

Continuing on in Genesis 1:26 God said *of* man...

"And let them have dominion..."

Finally, in verse 28, God said *to* man...

"Be fruitful, and multiply, and replenish the earth, and subdue it: and have dominion..."

The issuance of this divine decree in Genesis 1:28 was the official initiation of our destiny of dominion.

You don't have to be a biblical scholar who has read the Word from Genesis to Revelation to know about our destiny of dominion. This divine decree of dominion is in the very first chapter of the very first book of the Bible. It is the very first recorded words spoken by God *about* man, *of* man and *to* man.

The *"Law of First Mention"* or the *"Divine Law of Firsts"* is a principle which states that the first mention of a subject in the Word has special significance because it establishes an *unchangeable* pattern and *sets the stage* for how that subject is to be understood throughout the Word.

When God initially bequeathed dominion to Adam, Adam was ordained as the god of this world. However, Adam must not have fully grasped the magnitude of his delegated privilege and responsibility even though God's instructions were crystal clear. If he had, he would not have passed his baton of dominion to Satan, ordaining him as the god of this world (2 Corinthians 4:4).

I'm certain Adam could not have fathomed that this one "simple" act of disobedience would alter God's divine design for mankind and result in such a horrific series of events.

Unlike Adam, Satan fully grasped the magnitude of his delegated privilege and responsibility. If you recall, he fearlessly flaunted this pivotal transference of power during his attempt to tempt Jesus in the wilderness...

> "And he said to him, 'I will give you all their authority and splendor, *for it has been given to me*, and I can give it to anyone I want to. So if you worship me, it will all be yours.'"
>
> Luke 4: 6-7 NIV

Satan knew the potential of the power he already possessed as the god of this world, although illegally obtained. Adam had passed the baton of dominion to him and as such, he now had the authority to give that power to whomever he pleased…even Jesus. His sole request was for Jesus to worship *him*. In his mind, if he could pull this one off, he would authenticate his power and advance his position to be the master of the universe.

Both Jesus and Satan knew the stakes were high. If Jesus had complied with Satan's sole request, a multitude of souls would have been mortally impacted. While Satan's proposal appeared to be "the perfect solution" *for* Jesus, it most certainly did not sound like the perfect solution *to* Jesus.

Satan will always present us with a "quick fix" that appears appealing and sounds sweet but rest assured behind every perfect solution presented lurks an ulterior motive that is far more favorable to his cause than ours.

As the clichés say, "appearances can be deceiving" because "things aren't always as they appear to be".

Satan's lone requirement for this reciprocity of power was for Jesus to pay homage and worship him…just once.

Let the people of God say…

"Just Once Is All It Takes."

Just one "simple" act of disobedience can complicate an entire life…an entire family…an entire nation…an entire creation.

Jesus purposely abdicated His divinity to acquire humanity so that He could *terminate, not facilitate,* the works of the devil.

The plan of redemption was executed with precision and power to irrevocably reverse the curse and indisputably reinstate God's divine design for His people – a destiny of dominion. The plan of redemption predefined how this final transference of power would take place and Satan's "perfect solution" was most definitely not on the agenda.

What Satan did *not* fully grasp was that Jesus *was* the Perfect Solution.

The final transference of power, consummated at Calvary with the shedding of the precious blood of the Holy Lamb of God, deactivated and demolished Satan's illegally obtained power and reactivated and restored our God-given power!

Let the people of God say…

"I'VE GOT THE POWER!"

Sadly, Adam's decision of disobedience has had a ripple effect that has been detrimental to our ability to accept God's divine design and assume our rightful position to operate in our destiny of dominion.

Even today, although God is crystal clear in His instructions concerning the recovery and restoration of our dominion over **ALL** the earth, we do not fully grasp the magnitude of our delegated privilege and responsibility.

If we fully grasped the magnitude of our delegated privilege and responsibility, we would not continue to pass our baton of dominion to Satan through "simple" acts of disobedience that cause unnecessary delays and undesirable complications in our lives.

If we fully grasped the magnitude of our delegated privilege and responsibility, we would not be living powerless, pitiful and puny lives but productive, profitable and prosperous lives. We would be cultivating and conserving the wondrous works of God's hands. We would be exercising control and assuming absolute authority over **ALL** the earth, particularly the forces of evil in our life…not vice versa.

Jesus nullified the "vice versa" when He verified in Matthew 28:18 (NLT)…

"I have been given all authority in heaven and on earth."

What Satan did *not* fully grasp was the fact that Jesus was the Divine Alternative to the design alteration.

Our destiny of dominion was recovered from the hand of the enemy and restored to the people of God by the Son of God. By one man, our destiny of dominion was relinquished; by one Man our destiny of dominion was reclaimed.

Let the people of God say…

"I'VE GOT THE POWER!"

In 2004, millions of people flocked to theaters all across the world to see *"The Passion of the Christ"*, a powerful portrayal of the final hours and crucifixion of Jesus Christ. In North America, *"The Passion"* is the highest-grossing R-rated film of all time.

Resurrection Sunday, more familiarly known as Easter Sunday, begins a seven-week season called *"Eastertide"*, the Great Fifty Days, that commences at sundown the evening before Easter Sunday and lasts for six Sundays until Pentecost Sunday. These "Sundays of Easter" as they are called, climax on the seventh Sunday, Ascension Day, which is the week before Pentecost Sunday.

Resurrection Sunday is a commemoration of the story of the Glory. With adulation, we celebrate the virgin birth of the anointed Jesus. With admiration, we celebrate His virtuous life. With adoration, we celebrate His vicarious death. With appreciation, we celebrate His vowed resurrection. With anticipation, we celebrate His vibrant return and our victorious eternity.

But if we totally comprehended the epic essence of this sacred season, our commemoration of the story of the Glory would not be so finite. Instead, we would joyously commemorate this sacred season every day of every month, every month of every year.

For it was during this highly significant, most memorable season that Jesus gave His precious life to save ours. For our good to God's glory, Jesus was hung up for our hang ups.

For our good to God's glory, Jesus was hung up for our sin and our shame. He knew no sin but became sin and suffered shame so that through His precious shed blood, we could be made righteous in God's sight (2 Corinthians 5:21).

For our good to God's glory, Jesus was hung up for our sickness and our diseases. He knew no sickness but assumed all of our diseases so that through the wounds and bruises He endured, we could be healed, healthy and whole (1 Peter 2:24).

For our good to God's glory, Jesus was hung up for our poverty and our lack. Jesus knew no poverty but renounced His riches and acquired our lack so that through His poverty all of our debts could be expunged (2 Corinthians 8:9).

For our good to God's glory, Jesus satisfied the deficiency in **ALL** things and through His sacrifice, we can savor **ALL** sufficiency in **ALL** things (2 Corinthians 9:8).

For our good to God's glory, when God raised Jesus from the dead on that third day, we, who were dead in our transgressions and our sins were raised up and given joint-seating with Christ at the right hand of the throne of God (Ephesians 2:1, 5-6).

At the precise time God's resurrection power raised Jesus from the dead, He raised *every dead situation in our life*! God's resurrection power recovered and restored our dominion.

Christ, the Head of **ALL** principality and **ALL** power, stumped and trumped the wicked rulers of the darkness of this world, triumphantly disarmed and disgraced the principalities and powers, completely disrobing them of **ALL** power over us and delegated absolute authority to us over **ALL** the power of the enemy.

BUT…and yes, there is a "but"…it is up to *us* to exercise our God-given rights. Satan has *no* right or power to run rampant in our life. He has been stripped completely naked and is devoid of the power he illegally obtained from Adam in the Garden of Eden.

> *Satan is powerless;*
> *WE ARE POWERFUL!*

Let the people of God say…

"I'VE GOT THE POWER!"

The *only* power Satan has is the power that *we* give him. Why do we keep giving him power over our life? Is what he's promising us so much better than what we've already been promised?

Just once is all Satan needs. Just one "simple" act of disobedience to God's divine decrees passes our baton of dominion to him. As long as he continues to hold our baton of dominion, he will continue to wave it recklessly over our life. As long as He continues to wave *our* baton of dominion over *our* life, we will continue to live powerless, crisis-filled, complicated lives when our true calling is to live powerful, Christ-centered, simple lives.

Just imagine if you can, where we would be on this day if Jesus had taken Satan up on his proposal on that day. Imagine what Satan would have done *if* Jesus had taken the easy way out by snatching this "quick fix" and worshipping Satan…just once.

Do we really believe for one moment that Satan would have just turned everything over to Jesus…like he *said* he would?

Absolutely not!

"…for he is a liar, and the father of lies."

John 8:44 NLT

Satan would have turned right around and used the power that Jesus gave him against Him.

Oh but thank God for the story of the Glory! Thank God that the glory of the Lord was revealed in the Person of His only Son, Jesus, the Anointed Christ, who knew, believed and walked in His destiny of dominion.

Jesus didn't entertain Satan's indecent proposals. Why do we constantly open up ourselves through civil disobedience to entertain his indecent proposals?

We don't belong to Satan. Now are we the sons and daughters of God. We've been purchased at a premium price – the precious blood of the Holy Lamb of God. God rescued us from being dominated by darkness and rendered to us the power to dominate darkness (Colossians 1:13).

Let the people of God say…

"I'VE GOT THE POWER!"

People of God, we are kings and queens in the Kingdom of God. Who do you think are the kings that Christ is King of?

> **"But you are a chosen race, *a royal priesthood*, a dedicated nation, [God's] own purchased, special people…"**
> 1 Peter 2:9 AMP

We are members of the Royal Family of God…*and membership has its privileges.*

As heirs of God and joint-heirs with Christ, we have an incorruptible inheritance of life eternal and an existing, inexplicable inheritance of an abundant life of power, peace and prosperity.

As members of the Royal Family of God, it is *our* privilege and *our* responsibility to activate and exercise our destiny of dominion over the forces of evil in our life.

> *Royalty is not dominated;*
> *ROYALTY DOMINATES!*

When we open an account at a local bank, the bank issues us an ATM card that grants us unlimited access to the funds we have deposited into our account. When our ATM card is received by mail, a sticker is located across the top prompting us to call or go online to activate our card as soon as possible.

Why? Well, just having the ATM card in our possession doesn't automatically grant us access to our funds. Until we activate it, our ATM card is powerless. Once we activate it, our ATM card will grant us access to our funds anytime, anywhere ATM cards are accepted...provided we have sufficient funds deposited in our account.

Similarly, when we join the Royal Family of God, we are issued God's two very special ATM cards: 1) His **Awesome Tender Mercies** that grant us unlimited access to the Throne of Grace where Jesus has deposited His precious blood for the remission of our sins and 2) an **Anointing To Manifest** His promises in our life and live life by His divine design by operating in our destiny of dominion.

When we receive God's first ATM card in our spirit, it works automatically...continuously (1 Chronicles 16:34).

When we receive God's second ATM card in our spirit, it's up to us to go online – to get connected to the Throne of Grace where we can activate our destiny of dominion as soon as possible.

Just having this second ATM card in our possession doesn't automatically grant us access to our new powerful life *in Christ*. Until we activate our destiny of dominion, we remain powerless. Once we activate it, our ATM card will grant us access to the exceeding great and precious promises of God anytime, anywhere...provided we have sufficient faith and love deposited in our account.

Far too many members of the Royal Family of God are living in crisis and being dominated when our true calling is to live *in Christ* and dominate because we have failed to accept God's first ATM card in our life and activate God's second ATM card for our life.

Far too many members of the Royal Family of God are sitting in the waiting room waiting on God because...

1. They *don't know* that we've got the power or
2. They *don't believe* we've got the power or
3. They *don't work* the power we've got.

Not long ago, I purchased Verizon's first touch-screen BlackBerry, the Storm. I was excited about my shiny, new toy and wanted to get right to it. There were so many features on this phone that promised to streamline daily tasks to improve time management.

Truth be told, these "crackberries" as blackberries are affectionately known, though they *appear* to be a blessing in disguise, are nothing more than another deliberate distraction. If you have ever been in the presence of a friend or colleague with a blackberry in their hand, you know exactly what I'm talking about.

Well, after a couple of days of fiddling around with the phone, my excitement waned as I became frustrated because I was unable to figure out exactly how to work all the fabulous features on my new phone.

I called my son, Tyrique, who is a gadget guru, to ask him some questions about the features on *my* phone. (Mind you, he doesn't even own a BlackBerry Storm.) After listening patiently to my barrage of questions, his reply, though simple was very profound, *"I don't know but I always find it helpful to read the instructions."*

This is so typical of how we as believers operate. When we first received the free gift of salvation, we were all excited about our new life *in Christ* and the prospect of the manifestation of the promises of God in our life.

But for years, we've been spinning our wheels trying to figure things out on our own or asking other people's opinions about God's plan for *our* life or sitting in the waiting room waiting for God to do...*something else.*

At the end of the day, when we're between a rock and that hard place, we cry out, mumbling and grumbling and asking God all kinds of questions filled with unbelief when...I don't know...we just might find it helpful to read the instructions.

The Word of God is full of instructions for the people of God about how we should live our new life *in Christ* and "how to" receive the manifestation of God's promises in our life.

There was an article that was being circulated on the internet entitled *"Blacks Don't Read"* that insulted and infuriated many individuals in the black community. The opening sentence is *"They are still our slaves."* The premise of the article is...

. . . .

> *"Their IGNORANCE is the primary weapon of containment. A great man once said, 'The best way to hide something from Black people is to put it in a book.' We now live in the Information Age. They have gained the opportunity to read any book on any subject through the efforts of their fight for freedom, yet they refuse to read."*

. . . .

While there is *some* realism to this article, this blanket statement is definitely NOT an absolute truth for all Black people.

There are plenty of Black people who have taken full advantage of the opportunities that have been afforded us by the demeaning and dreadful sacrifices made by our ancestors as well as the successive trailblazers whose ambitious spirits have allowed them to experience unprecedented success.

As I pondered this article, I began to parallel its premise to the current state of the Royal Family of God – the body of Christ.

I paraphrase the above paragraph to show the uncanny similarity.

> *"Their IGNORANCE is the primary weapon of containment. A great Man once said, 'My people are destroyed for lack of knowledge.' We now live in the Information Age. Even if they don't physically own a Bible, electronic versions in multiple translations can be found on the worldwide web. They have been given the free gift of salvation through the sacrifice of Jesus, the Christ, and have been given instructions about how to live victoriously in this life, yet they refuse to read."*

While there is *some* realism to this quote, this blanket statement is definitely NOT an absolute truth for all the members of the Royal Family of God. Make no mistake; there are multitudes of the Royal Family living like royalty – living life by divine design *in Christ*. But is it possible that many Christians are living in crisis because *"Christians Don't Read"* the instructions or that many believers are living life by default because *"Believers Don't Believe"* God's Word?

As in the opening sentence of the original article, Satan boldly and loudly proclaims to his cohorts *"They are still our slaves"*.

> *We've become COMFORTABLE being UNCOMFORTABLE.*

Our ignorance regarding our destiny of dominion has left us in a state of complacency in our cataclysmic circumstances.

Ignorance keeps us estranged from the Prince of Peace and enslaved to the prince of darkness allowing him to continually dominate us when it is our destiny to dominate him.

We've been under the influence of darkness for so long that unless we spend quality time immersed in God's Word allowing the light of His Word to shine brightly in our hearts, we will continue to be entangled with the yoke of bondage and be dominated all our life...until Jesus returns.

> **"The entrance of thy words giveth light; it giveth understanding unto the simple."**
> **Psalm 119:130**

As we allow the light of God's Word to penetrate our hearts, the Holy Spirit will illuminate our minds to the indisputable reality that God's divine design for His people is to have dominion and not be dominated and the irrefutable truth that God delivered us from the power of darkness to restore us to our rightful place of dominion.

Let the people of God say...

"I'VE GOT THE POWER!"

Let's briefly examine the three types of believers that are sitting in the waiting room waiting for God to do...*something else*.

The first believer doesn't even know who we *really* are; they don't know that we are Royalty. They don't know that we have power over **ALL** the power of the enemy. This group of believers falls under the *"Christians Don't Read"* category. Again, you don't have to be a biblical scholar who has read the Word from cover to cover to know about our destiny of dominion. The divine decree of dominion is the very first recorded words spoken by God about man, of man and to man in the very first chapter of the very first book of the Bible.

Contrary to the commonly quoted maxim, *"What you don't know can't hurt you"*, what these believers don't know hurts and hinders them from operating in our destiny of dominion.

Listen, if we don't know our rights, we have no rights. If we don't take the time to read God's Word to get to know who God really is and what He's done for us *in Christ*, we will never receive what's rightfully ours in this life. If we don't meditate on His Word to get to know who *we* really are *in Christ*, what we can do *through Christ*, where we can go *with Christ*, we will never operate in our destiny of dominion.

Now realize this…lack of knowledge does not negate the availability of God's promises to us but it does neutralize our ability to receive God's promises. It also grants the enemy, the chief thief, easy access to steal from us what God has promised to us.

Lack of knowledge is an obstruction of justice. Jesus paid an awesome price for a debt He didn't owe that we might be justified. Being made just *in Christ*, God bestowed on us precious promises. But it is up to us to appropriate these exceedingly great and precious promises into our life. How?

> **"…by coming to know him, the one who called us to himself by means of his marvelous glory and excellence."**
>
> **2 Peter 1:3 NLT**

Lack of knowledge of who God really is obstructs the just from appropriating what God has already done in our life. We can never know who *we really* are *in Christ* and what God has done for us *in Christ* if we don't know who God really is.

Until they acquire and apply this knowledge, this group of believers is doomed to suffer an identity crisis and live life by default.

The second believer knows the Word but doesn't believe what they know. This group of believers falls under the *"Believers Don't Believe"* category. Out of the three, this category is where the vast majority of believers fit in. As I mentioned at the outset, this book is written to a select group of born-again believers – *believers who believe God*.

Believe it or not, most believers don't believe God. They may believe *in* God but they really don't believe God. Even in the early days of the church, *"some believed the things which were spoken, and some believed not"* (Acts 28:24).

You see, it's not enough just "to know" the Word. Satan knows God's Word...but his knowledge is limited. He does not have and cannot receive revelation knowledge because he is spiritually dead and revelation knowledge is spiritually discerned (1 Corinthians 2:14).

Here's the clincher...not only does Satan know God's Word, Satan *believes* God's Word.

That's why he works relentlessly to put a twist on God's Word so he can twist the minds of God's people.

It's a shame to say but Satan probably knows how to work God's Word...in his favor, of course...better than many of God's people know how to work the Word in their life. That's why identity theft has been so successful in the body of Christ.

The Word will do the work if we learn how to work the Word. The key to working the Word is believing the Word.

Jesus says in Mark 9:23...

> **"*If thou canst believe*, all things are possible to him that believeth."**

That is so powerful! He didn't say *some* things are possible, He said **ALL** things are possible *if* we can believe. Do you know what else that means? That means that *nothing is impossible* to us.

That's deep.

The thing about this spiritual principle is it works both ways. It works however *we* work it – positively or negatively. The problem is, because of their cardiac condition, most believers work this powerful principle negatively – against themselves.

Earlier I shared that our casual conversation is a reflection of our cardiac condition.

If you listen closely to the conversation of most "believers", you will hear just how much unbelief is in their hearts. In fact, there is probably more unbelief in their hearts than there is belief.

In reality, this unbelief is belief in the wrong story. So to be clear, there is more unbelief in the Word of God in their hearts than there is belief in the Word of God.

One of the main reasons God's people are not receiving is because God's people are not believing.

> **"Therefore I tell you, whatever you ask for in prayer, *believe that you have received it*, and it will be yours."**
> **Mark 11:24 NIV**

"Seeing is believing" is a popular idiom that means unless I am shown convincing concrete evidence, I won't believe what you tell me. You've probably heard someone say or maybe have even said it yourself, *"I'll believe it when I see it"*.

Satan has purposely programmed the world's thinking this way because he knows that in the Word, "believing is seeing". He knows that the people of God receive the things of God when they believe God… even before they've seen a thing.

> **"NOW FAITH is the assurance (the confirmation, the title deed) of the things [we] hope for, *being the proof of things [we] do not see* and the conviction of their reality [faith perceiving as real fact what is not revealed to the senses]."**
> **Hebrews 11:1 AMP**

FAITH IS our concrete evidence that we have received what God has promised. Faith acts "as if" God's promises are already real because faith knows God's promises *are* already real.

One of Jesus' own disciples, Thomas, refused to believe his fellow disciples when they spoke of Jesus' post-resurrection visitations…

> **"Unless I see…I will not believe it."**
>
> **John 20:25 NIV**

The truth of the matter is unless we BELIEVE it, we will never SEE it.

Doubting Thomas still lives in the body of Christ today – always waiting to "see it" before they'll believe it.

> **"Then Jesus told him, 'Because you have seen me, you have believed;** *blessed are those who have not seen and yet have believed.'"*
>
> John 20:29 NIV

By faith, Noah believed God's promise that He would destroy every living creature on the earth and built an ark on dry land according to God's specifications even before he saw one drop of rain. He acted on what he was told about something he had not yet seen.

By faith, Abraham believed God's promise that He would make him the father of many nations but built an altar on Mt. Moriah according to God's word to sacrifice his promised son Isaac even before he saw his first grandchild. He acted on what he was told about something he had not yet seen.

Faith believes before it sees.

Unbelief is an insult to God. After all He's done for us, how can we still not trust that He has our best interest at heart or believe that He would ever do anything that would put us in harm's way? After all He's done for us, why do we still choose to believe the wrong story rather than believe the story of the Glory? After all He's done for us, why are we still waiting for Him to do *something else* before we'll believe?

Although unbelief has never, can never and will never change the ability of God's Word to work, be very sure that unbelief can and *will* prevent God's Word from working in the life of the "unbeliever".

The third believer knows *and* believes but doesn't apply the Word – they don't work the Word. You know, Satan really doesn't care if we know the Word because like I said before, he knows the Word. He doesn't even really care if we believe the Word...he believes the Word. But he will get a little agitated when a believer who knows and believes the Word *acts* on the Word! That, for him, is a huge problem.

The practical three-step course of action contained in this book has the power to change what happens **NEXT** in your life – depending on your own personal course of *action*.

The famed Italian painter, Leonardo da Vinci once said…

*"I have been impressed with
the urgency of doing.
Knowing is not enough, we must apply.
Being willing is not enough, we must do."*

James, the brother of Jesus, says it this way…

"Faith without works is dead."
James 2:26

Dead faith is alive and living in the body of Christ. Either because believers are not acting on their faith or if they are acting on their faith, they're not walking in love (Galatians 5:6).

* PAUSE & PONDER *

There are more disciples sitting *in* the boat (aka "the waiting room") watching the "Peters" who got out of the boat and are walking on water than there are water-walking "Peters".

Why is that?

Well, we already know some believers are sitting *in* the boat because they're waiting for God to do *something else* but there are still other believers who choose to stay in the boat simply because of comfortable inaction.

Yes, they have big dreams and strong desires to do something different, something more satisfying that requires them to get out of the boat and walk on the water but sitting in the boat, however uncomfortable it may be, is way more comfortable than believing God and venturing out of their comfort zone.

So they choose to be spectators…not participators…ever so patiently waiting to pounce when the water-walking "Peters" begin to sink to justify their choice to stay in the boat. They dismiss the fact that these "Peters" walked on water in the first place.

People of God, like the children of Israel, we're going somewhere we've never been and we may have to do some things we've never done and go through some things we've never been through. But the only way we're going to be able to get where we're going and do what God wants us to do is to *believe God*.

Prior to this miraculous incident, there is no place in the Word we find Peter walking on water. Why? Peter had never walked on water before. The reason Peter got out of that boat and walked on the water was because He believed God.

> **"Lord, if it is You, command me to come to You on the water."**
> **Matthew 14:28 AMP**

Jesus said, *"Come"* and Peter went. In modern terminology, Jesus said *"Let's"* and Peter said *"Go!"*

Jesus spoke the word; Peter heard the word, believed the word and acted on the word he heard. Peter remembered the day when after fishing all night long without catching a thing, Jesus came and commanded him to let down his nets again…

> "Master, we've worked hard all night and haven't caught anything. *But because you say so*, I will let down the nets."
>
> Luke 5:5 NIV

And when he did what Jesus *said* to do…

> "…they caught such a large number of fish that their nets began to break."
>
> Luke 5:6 NIV

Once again in a boat, Peter took God at His word because he believed God. What Peter did that day is called *applied* faith.

The late Dr. Martin Luther King once said…

*"Take the first step in faith.
You don't have to see the whole staircase,
just take the first step."*

For years, we've been trained to believe that "knowledge is power"; the supposition being the more knowledge we have the more power we have.

Well, clearly this cliché is faulty. Most believers "know" what to do yet they are still living powerless lives. If knowing was truly enough, every believer "in the know" would be living in a constant flow that life by divine design affords.

The reality is knowledge is only *potential* power. It's not about knowing what to do; it's about *doing* what you know. Like Nike's infamous slogan compels us…

"JUST DO IT!"

If we want to experience the avalanche of abundance God has blessed us with *in Christ* and the blizzard of blessings that are ours as heirs of God and joint-heirs with Christ Jesus, we've got to show what we know in our actions.

> "...don't just listen to God's word. *You must do what it says.* Otherwise, you are only fooling yourselves."
>
> **James 1:22 NLT**

Let the people of God say…

"IF YOU WANT TO WALK ON WATER YOU'VE GOT TO GET OUT OF THE BOAT."

Today I plugged the phrase "self-help" in Google and got 436,000,000 hits. That's four hundred thirty six *million* hits of resources about improving low self-esteem, spiritual growth, personal transformation, success motivation, stress management, etc. When I plugged in the phrase "self-help seminars", I got six million, ten thousand hits. Depending on their popularity, these self-proclaimed self-help writers and speakers charge exorbitant fees for their "expert advice" about "how to" improve *your* life.

What's so amazing to me is that so many believers, present company included, have read these books and magazines and attended these seminars when in one chapter of one Book (Joshua 1:8), God has *already* given us the secret to our success. God has *already* told us "how to" do what we need to do to get what He's *already* given us.

> "**Study this Book of Instruction continually. Meditate on it day and night so you will be sure to obey everything written in it.** *Only then* **will you prosper and succeed in all you do.**"

From God's mouth to our ears, there is *only one way* we will walk in our destiny of dominion and live life by His divine design.

Study the Word, meditate on the Word and follow the instructions in the Word…continually, not conveniently.

MEDITATION DETERMINES REVELATION

A common misconception among believers is that reading and meditating are one in the same. They are not. Many believers read the Bible, mostly during corporate scripture reading in church or sometimes in the midst of an impending dangerous situation but very few believers meditate on the words they have read.

Just reading a passage of scripture once or twice doesn't necessarily mean it will make a lasting impression on our mind or spirit.

Meditation involves intently reflecting on what was read then intentionally engaging our mind to allow what we've read to marinate until it saturates our spirit.

Acquiring the wisdom of God is the wisest acquisition one can make. The wisdom of God is in the Word of God. We acquire the wisdom of God as we meditate on His Word. Equally essential to acquiring the wisdom of God is acquiring revelation knowledge – understanding (Proverbs 4:7).

> **"You made me; you created me. Now give me the sense to follow your commands."**
>
> **Psalm 119:73 NLT**

The end result of prayerful and purposeful meditation where our spirit becomes more receptive to the voice of our Guidance Counselor, the Holy Spirit, is powerful revelation.

REVELATION DEMANDS APPLICATION

God chooses how and when He responds to our prayers. He may speak to us in a still small voice or He may send a word of confirmation through a chosen vessel. He may point us to specific passages of scripture that speak specifically to our life experience at that moment in time.

Have you ever received a word from the Lord in the still of the night that was an answer to a particular request you had before the Lord? Has anyone ever shared a personal experience that encouraged you to hold on? Have you ever been reading a familiar passage of scripture that *this time* seemed to speak directly to your situation?

In spite of what many people believe, God always answers prayer. The key to receiving the answer is fine-tuning our reception, which comes through consistent prayerful and purposeful meditation. If our reception is off-kilter, we won't be able to clearly hear from God. As a result, most believers just assume that God has not answered their prayer.

Then there are those times when we audibly hear from God but disregard His voice because the answer He gave wasn't the answer we were expecting to receive.

Instead of assuming our responsibility to apply what He's revealed (if that's what He's told us to do) we flip it back and say, *"Well, I'll just leave it in God's hands"*. So we sit in the waiting room – you know, to give God time to think things over – and wait patiently for Him to say…*something else*.

Once revelation knowledge is received, if God instructs us to apply what He's revealed, then we must apply what He's revealed.

Application Delivers Manifestation

It is my humble belief that a delay in the manifestation of God's promises in our life can be traced back to a delinquency in application. And what many believers have done to justify these delays is accept them as denials. *"Well, it must not be the will of God."*

But according to the instructions in Joshua 1:8, application of the revelation received in meditation *will* always produce the manifestation.

> **"Heaven and earth shall pass away but My words shall not pass away."**
> **Matthew 24:35**

The Word promises that God will do immeasurably more…the *Amplified* version of Ephesians 3:20 says *"far over and above all that we [dare] ask or think [infinitely beyond our highest prayers, desires, thoughts, hopes, or dreams]"*…according to His power that is at work within us.

Every promise God has made to us already belongs to us but we must activate that power by plugging into and staying securely connected to the Power Source if we are to possess those promises.

God is not slack concerning His promise. Everything He said He would do, He's already done.

King's Solomon's prayer of dedication after the building of the Temple was…

> **"O LORD, God of Israel, there is no God like you in heaven above or on earth below—you who *keep your covenant of love* with your servants who continue wholeheartedly in your way. You have kept your promise to your servant David my father; *with your mouth you have promised and with your hand you have fulfilled it*—as it is today."**
>
> **1 Kings 8:23-24 NIV**

King Solomon goes on to say in verse 56...

> **"Praise be to the LORD, who has given rest to his people Israel just as he promised.** *Not one word has failed of all the good promises he gave* **through his servant Moses."**

Let the people of God say...

"GOD IS A PROMISE-KEEPING GOD!"

As a member of the Royal Family of God, we are privy to His good promises of power, peace and prosperity *in Christ.*

God's promise of peace in Isaiah 26:3 (NLT) is intended for a mind focused on trusting the power of His Word.

> **"You will keep in perfect peace all who trust in you, all whose thoughts are fixed on you!"**

So many believers are staggering at the promises when we should be standing on the promises in the Word because our thoughts are more focused on the pandemonium in the world.

Our focus determines our direction in our life. If our focus is on the pandemonium in the world, the reality we create is a life filled with pressure and confusion. If our focus is on the promises in the Word, the reality we create is a life filled with peace and confidence. That's certainly not to say that everyday will be peaceful but the peace of God will surpass and supersede the pressure and confusion and...

> **"Before you know it, a sense of God's wholeness, everything coming together for good, will come and settle you down. It's wonderful what happens when Christ displaces worry at the center of your life."**
>
> **Philippians 4:7 MSG**

God's promise of peace in Isaiah 26:3 is extended to a mind that is fully persuaded that there is life and power in God's Word that never changes…but has the power to change life.

God's promise of prosperity in Joshua 1:8 corroborates His promise of peace in Isaiah 26:3 which corroborates His promise of power in 2 Timothy 1:7.

God's promises of power, peace and prosperity all relate to our state of mind. That's why it is so crucial that we be transformed by renewing our minds because letting our sinful nature control our minds only leads to death.

> **"But letting the Spirit control your mind leads to life and peace."**
>
> **Romans 8:6 AMP**

Before we were born-again, our state of mind was sinful and hostile toward God. The enemy wants to keep us in this sinful state of mind because he knows that if we maintain that mindset, we will *never* receive God's promises.

Transformation precedes Transition.

Before we can make that transition to our land of Promise, we've got to transform our thinking. We can't get where we're going without changing what we're thinking.

> **"…the sinful mind is hostile to God. It does not submit to God's law, nor can it do so."**
>
> **Romans 8:7 NIV**

Allowing our sinful mind to reign and rule leads to death. Allowing the Spirit to transform our mind leads to life and peace.

> *Transformation precedes Translation.*

Before we can translate what God has been saying to us in His Word, we've got to transform our thinking. Otherwise what God is saying will all seem like nonsense.

> **"...people who aren't spiritual can't receive these truths from God's Spirit. It all sounds foolish to them and they can't understand it, for only those who are spiritual can understand what the Spirit means."**
> **1 Corinthians 2:14 NLT**

Right now, many believers are lost in transition because something was lost in translation because there has been no transformation.

Believers have been hypnotized by the snake charmer and are unwilling to exchange the glam and glitter this world has to offer for the grace and glory the Word has to offer.

The body of Christ – like the fallen angels and Eve and the children of Israel – have given up everything they already have...for what Satan has to offer.

Transformation only comes through divine connection. The reason we've been deliberately distracted about our destiny of dominion is because we have not been divinely connected.

Only when we make a consistent and persistent effort to get and stay *securely* divinely connected to the Power Source will we receive deliverance from Satan's deliberate distractions and operate successfully in our destiny of dominion.

Divine Connection

Everything God did, He did by design. From the creation to the crucifixion, from the resurrection to redemption, everything that was done was done by design.

From the very beginning of time, the essence of God's divine design has been about divine connections – the connection of the Father, Son and Holy Ghost; the connection of the grass to the earth; the connection of the sun to the moon; the connection of the fish to the sea; the connection of the birds to the sky. Adam was connected to God and Eve was connected to Adam.

Divine connections play an integral part in the Master's magnificent orchestration of the symphony of our life.

God's divine design for His children to operate successfully in our destiny of dominion and live an abundant life of power, peace and prosperity in this life and life eternal is only accessible through divine connection.

The creation is a dazzling depiction of the mighty splendor and majestic sovereignty of our Creator. His impeccable innovative skills and astute attention to detail are clearly a public display of His affection toward His creation.

We are the apple of His eye (Zechariah 2:8).

Prior to the fall, the life of Adam and Eve was the epitome of life by divine design that God had in mind. Eden was a place of totality – a place where *nothing* was missing and *nothing* was broken.

Everything Adam and Eve needed to live an abundant life of power, peace and prosperity was provided for them…as long as they stayed divinely connected to God. As long as they remained in the light of His glory, they lived life by His divine design.

Divine connection is the provision to the provision of the divine design.

The Master Design: Step One

Divine connection is the stipulation to living God's provision of an abundant life of power, peace and prosperity.

When the divine design was altered through Eve's deception and Adam's disobedience, the divine connection was severed, life by design for them ceased and life by default commenced.

The light of God's glory that was in them and on them, dissipated...and the struggle began.

> *The struggle always begins...*
> *where the light ends.*

Oh but thank God that the glory of God was restored to the people of God by the Word of God, the Anointed Jesus. The divine design was reinstated when Jesus exchanged His life for ours. This selfless exchange eradicated life by default that was introduced by Satan in the garden and elevated life by divine design that was initiated by God in the beginning!

JESUS IS the Divine Connection to God's divine design.

> **"I am the Way, the Truth, and the Life: no one comes to the Father except by (through) me."**
>
> **John 14:6 AMP**

JESUS IS our ONLY Way to God. Staying divinely connected to Him keeps us divinely connected to God.

> **"I and my Father are one."**
>
> **John 10:30**

JESUS IS the ONLY Truth. Staying divinely connected to Him consecrates and liberates us.

> "Sanctify them [purify, consecrate, separate them for Yourself, make them holy] by the Truth; Your Word is Truth...and the Truth will set you free."
>
> John 17:17; John 8:32 AMP

JESUS IS the ONLY Life Light. Staying divinely connected to Him illuminates our journey along this pathway of life.

> "I am the Light of the world. He who follows Me will not be walking in the dark, but will have the Light which is Life."
>
> John 8:12 AMP

Simply put...staying divinely connected to Jesus, the Word of God, is the ONLY way to live life by divine design. Contrary to popular belief, there is no other way.

The sophistication of our physical anatomy dictates that, if we are to operate effectively and efficiently, our body must be securely connected to our head. Our body is designed to function in conjunction with our head. This is one connection that never has been (and I suppose never will be) second-guessed because the ramifications of disconnection are obvious – headless bodies become lifeless bodies. Our body cannot properly function without our head just as our head cannot properly function without our body.

As simplistic as this may sound, this very same *"concept"* applies to the sophistication of our spiritual anatomy which dictates that, if we are to operate effectively and efficiently, the body of Christ must be securely connected to the Head, which is Christ. The body is designed to function in conjunction with the Head.

Why, then, is *this* divine connection second-guessed when the exact same premise applies?

A glimpse at the current state of the body of Christ as a whole will confirm the reality that Headless bodies are lifeless bodies. The body of Christ cannot properly function without our Head just as our Head cannot properly function without His body.

Sadly, as we continue to digress from our intrinsic dependency on our Head, we have become dangerously independent. We have become progressively more dependent on our own strength and ability to handle the happenings in our daily life. Need we be reminded that the power we've been given by Christ only comes through a divine connection to Christ?

If we, God's people, want God to intervene and make an irreversible impact on the perilous issues we encounter in our lives – regionally, nationally and globally, we must heed God's solution to this situation in 2 Chronicles 7:14 (NIV)...

> **"If my people, who are called by my name, will humble themselves and pray and seek my face and turn from their wicked ways, then will I hear from heaven and will forgive their sin and will heal their land."**

The body of Christ is in a state of disarray because we've been deceived by our own pride. We took great pride in our positions and our possessions and in the wake of this mercantile meltdown which resulted in the dissolution of several mammoth corporations and firms, who once boasted astronomical profits, not only do we clearly see the remnants of pride as humiliation saturates our society, we have become casualties of our pride.

> **"Pride goes before destruction, and a haughty spirit before a fall."**
> **Proverbs 16:18 AMP**

God resists the proud...but gives grace to the humble (James 4:6). Acknowledgment of our need for God's Divine intervention is the first act of humility. Acceptance of His amazing grace is the final act of humility. Only when we humble ourselves under the mighty power of the Almighty Power will He lift us up and honor us at the appointed time (1 Peter 5:6).

As King Solomon so wisely states…

> **"A man's pride will bring him low, but he who is of a humble spirit will obtain honor."**
>
> **Proverbs 29:23 AMP**

The body of Christ is in a state of distress because we have sorely underrated the power in prayer. Hannah prayed for a son and the Lord granted her what she asked of Him (1 Samuel 1:27). Elisha prayed for a child to be raised from the dead *"and the child sneezed seven times…and opened his eyes"* (2 Kings 4:35). *"And the LORD turned the captivity of Job, when he prayed for his friends"* (Job 42:10). Daniel prayed and God sent an angel to shut the lions' mouth (Daniel 6:22).

Jesus prayed and God's will was done (Luke 22:42).

> **"The earnest prayer of a righteous person has great power and produces wonderful results."**
>
> **James 5:16 NLT**

We have been given this great privilege of prayer to connect us to the One Who sees everything and knows everything there is to know about everything and yet we fail to avail ourselves of the indomitable power in prayer.

The body of Christ is dysfunctional because we're delusional. We diligently seek after that which is unholy and ungodly in the world yet still expect to reap the rewards of those who diligently seek God.

> **"Seek the Kingdom of God above all else, and live righteously, and he will give you everything you need."**
>
> **Matthew 6:33 NLT**

What the body of Christ needs most is a *secure* divine connection to our Head. But that can't happen until we earnestly seek God, until our soul thirsts for Him and our body longs for Him in this dry and weary land, where there is no water; until we diligently seek to bask in His presence to behold His beauty all the days of our life.

As the intensity of our desire for more of Him magnifies and our propensity to follow His way of doing and being right multiplies, our divine connection to the Power Source will solidify and God will be glorified as we live life by His divine design.

But if we don't set aside our pride and turn from doing our own thing our own way all day every day, we can expect to continue to live a crisis-filled life dominated by evil forces because our divine connection from the Power Source will remain short-circuited or severed.

"The Lord will destroy the house of the proud..."

Proverbs 15:25

Jesus places paramount priority on divine connection in His parallel in John 15:5 (MSG)...

"I am the Vine, you are the branches. When you're joined with me and I with you, the relation intimate and organic, the harvest is sure to be abundant. *Separated, you can't produce a thing."*

Divine connection is not a one-way street. When we are joined with Christ in a purely, intimate relationship, Christ is joined with us in a purely, intimate relationship. Intimacy in a relationship generally has a sexual connotation but this intimacy we speak of and seek to obtain transcends the microscopic, restricted physical sensual association.

An intimate One-on-one relationship with Christ speaks to *developing* our deep-seated desire to be connected to the Core of our existence. Although the deviation from the divine design disengaged us from the divine connection, our innate desire remains intact and our subliminal self seeks re-connection.

This underlying and undeveloped desire to be intimately connected to Jesus is equally as strong as His unfaltering and unconditional desire to be intimately connected to us.

Even so, we foolishly continue to gravitate away from getting divinely connected to the Word to being defiantly connected to the world. An informal assessment of the life of the average believer would, more likely than not, prove that more "believers" are more securely connected to the world than to the Word.

We've often heard people make the comment that *"something is missing"* in their life. Their assessment is absolute. That something – or more appropriately *"Someone"* that is missing from their life is their Source of Life.

In the enlightening words of St. Augustine…

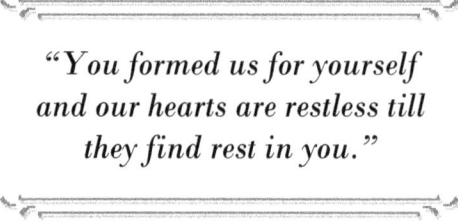

"You formed us for yourself and our hearts are restless till they find rest in you."

As the fish were created to be connected to the water and the plants to the soil, man was created to be divinely connected to God.

Disconnection from God can be likened to a fish out of water or a plant without soil. What happens when fish are out of water for an extended period of time? They will eventually suffocate and die as a result of being disconnected from their source of life. What happens when plants are taken out of the soil for an extended period of time? Their roots will eventually shrivel up and die as a result of being disconnected from their source of life.

What happens when a portrait is removed from its frame? Huh? We are portraits of God created to live within His framework. When a portrait is removed from its frame for an extended period of time, it eventually gets crumpled and crinkled, ripped and rolled, its edges become frayed and the portrait eventually fades.

Disconnection from our Source of Life results in spiritual death. As spiritual beings, our spiritual health is driven by our divine connection to our Source of Life. Our spiritual health is the dynamic force that drives our physical and mental health.

God promised Adam in Genesis 2:17 that they would surely die if they ate of the tree of the knowledge of good and evil. In due course, they experienced natural death but instantaneously they experienced spiritual death.

Because they severed their divine connection to their Source of Life, between the time of their spiritual demise and their natural demise, Adam and Eve experienced a life filled with crisis.

Disconnection from our Source of Life will always, beyond a shadow of a doubt, create a life filled with crisis.

You may or may not view your life as one filled with *"crisis"* but rest assured, any life lived short of God's divine design of an abundant life of power, peace and prosperity that comes through divine connectivity – is a life of mediocrity. A life of mediocrity produces a life of limited choices. A life of limited choices produces a life of crisis.

When we stay divinely connected to the Anointed One – we stay *in God's flow*. Overflow is inevitable *in God's flow*. There is no mediocrity *in Christ* – excellent is His name. There are no limited choices *in Christ* – only infinite riches. There is no crisis *in Christ*.

Equally, apart from us, Jesus' ability to work through us is impeded. We are the lanterns through which His Life Light shines. How much light can a lamp emit if it is not connected to the Power Source?

Staying divinely connected to the Power Source ensures that the Life Light shines. When the Life Light is shining through us, we will live life by divine design because the struggle always ends…where the Light begins.

As branches, producing a bountiful harvest is directly related to the security of our divine connection with the Vine. If we are not securely connected to Christ, we *will not* produce an abundant harvest because we *can not* produce an abundant harvest. It is impossible for the branch to be separated from the Vine and produce fruit.

> **"Remain in me, and I will remain in you. For a branch cannot produce fruit if it is severed from the vine, and you cannot be fruitful unless you remain in me."**
>
> **John 15:4 NLT**

In the same vein, if the branches are not securely connected to the Vine, the Vine has no suitable channel to properly produce the abundant harvest of God's glorious infinite riches.

Proverbs 12:12 tells us that *"the root of the righteous yields fruit."* This passage of scripture validates God's divine decree of our dominion in Genesis 1:28 where He commanded us to live fruitful lives. But in order for us to produce fruit, "our root" must be connected to *"The Root"*, the Anointed Jesus.

Disconnection from the Root yields no production of fruit. The fruit will be rotten if the Root is forgotten.

Jesus promises that if we abide in Him (dwell with Him, remain in Him and stay connected to Him) and allow His words to abide in us (dwell with us, remain in us and stay connected to us) that we can be sure that whatever we ask would be done for us (John 15:7).

A secure connection to the Divine Vine of Love produces a fruitful – productive, profitable and prosperous – life. A severed connection from the Divine Vine of Love produces a fruitless – powerless, pitiful and puny – life.

Collectively, born-again believers comprise the body of Christ. We are all divinely connected. Individually, each of us are members in particular of the body of Christ (1 Corinthians 12:27).

Our initial connection with the Divine Vine of Love and induction into the body of Christ occurs when we voice our choice to make Jesus our personal Savior and Lord in accordance with Romans 10:9. However, it is our individual responsibility to ensure that our connection stays secure by establishing an intimate One-on-one relationship with the Divine Vine so that we can be rooted and grounded in His love.

Many believers have delegated the responsibility for their spiritual health to the leaders in the body of Christ – Apostles, Prophets, Evangelists, Pastors and Teachers – who have been called to instruct the people of God in the things of God. Yes, these shepherds have delegated responsibility for feeding God's sheep but at the end of the day, the sheep are responsible for making sure that what we're being fed – the meat we eat – is proper nutrition for our spiritual condition.

What many believers fail to realize is there still exists an individual responsibility because when it's all said and done, there exists an individual accountability.

"Yes, each of us will give a personal account to God."

Romans 14:12 NIV

Naturally speaking, as members of this secular society, we are required to take accountability for the individual choices we make in our life and contributions we make to our society. Our point of reference for making such choices and contributions is the life lessons we learn as we sojourn. Every choice and every contribution we make impacts our life as well as our society in one way or another.

Spiritually speaking, as members of the body of Christ, we are required to take accountability for the individual choices we make in our life and the contributions we make to the body. Our point of reference for making these choices and contributions is the spiritual life lessons we learn as we sojourn. Every choice and every contribution we make impacts our life as well as the body of Christ in one way or another.

As members of the body, the level of intimacy in our personal love affair with the Divine Vine of Love makes a direct impact on the level of intimacy in our public love affair with Him.

Our ability to function effectively collectively as the body of Christ is completely dependent on our commitment to fulfilling our individual responsibility as members of the body of Christ.

As a Praise and Worship Leader, I have to tell you what a challenge it is ushering in the presence of God to a spiritually-dead congregation. God's presence is present in our praise. Because their relationship with God is not intimate, their praise and worship experience with God is inanimate.

Members of the body of Christ who do not have an intimate One-on-one relationship with the Divine Vine of Love undoubtedly are engaged in a different type of relationship that does not make it conducive for them to worship God for Who He is and praise Him for what He's done in their life.

Their lack of a personal love connection with the Divine Vine of Love dampens and hampers the collective praise and worship experience. Oh but thank God for the Anointing!

Let the people of God say...

"THE ANOINTING MAKES THE DIFFERENCE!"

Adherence to God's command in Joshua 1:8 steadily secures our connection to the Divine Vine of Love so that we can readily worship and praise our Holy Father for His Divine Love.

Paul persuades us in Philippians 2:2 (NIV) to be *"like-minded, having the same love, being one in spirit and purpose."* As Christians, if having Christ in our life has made a difference, our ultimate heart's desire should be to assertively and attentively develop an intimate One-on-one relationship with Him – a private love connection that overflows into our public love affair with Him.

Divine connection is the master key that unlocks the door to living life by divine design.

In the midst of this dark and dismal economy, we won't be shaken or stirred if we are securely connected to the Divine Vine of Love. Being securely connected transforms our thinking and renews our mind.

Up until now we've filled our minds with the world's way of thinking. Right now, the world is looking for hope in the midst of this economic earthquake and many folks have come to the conclusion that there is no hope.

For many believers, hope in the world's system has short-circuited their divine connection to the Life Light; just a minuscule glimmer of hope in the Word keeps their head above water. For others, hope in the world's system has completely severed their divine connection to the Life Light, and subsequently they live in crisis because the struggle always begins where the Light ends.

Hope in the world brings hopelessness.

But we have a blessed assurance in Psalm 146:5 (NIV)...

"Blessed is he whose help is the God of Jacob, whose hope is in the LORD his God."

As the songwriter Edward Mote wrote..."*My hope is built on nothing less than Jesus' blood and righteousness...On Christ the Solid Rock I stand all other ground is sinking sand.*"

This well-loved hymn has withstood the test of time. As we survey the domino effect that this economic earthquake has imposed in this world, we realize that **ALL** other ground...*has sunk.*

But the Word of the Lord declares in Isaiah 40:8 (NLT)...

"The grass withers and the flowers fade, but the word of our God stands forever."

Like Abraham, right in the midst of this mess, against hope we can still have hope in God's Word. When our natural hope expires, our supernatural hope should inspire (Romans 4:18).

Like David, we can have a *yet* praise because God's Word is our source of hope (Psalm 42:11; Psalm 119:114).

Their most hopeless situations seemed hopeful because clearly Abraham and David maintained a secure divine connection with God.

> **"'Abraham believed God, and God counted him as righteous because of his faith.' He was even called the friend of God."**
>
> James 2:23 NLT

Can you imagine God calling you His friend? **I CAN!** How did Abraham earn such a distinguishable title? He kept his divine connection secure by developing and maintaining an intimate One-on-one relationship with God that ultimately enabled him to believe God in a truly unbelievable situation.

> **"I have found David son of Jesse, a man after my own heart. He will do everything I want him to do."**
>
> Acts 13:22 NLT

One of the most fascinating things about David was his appreciation of the magnitude of his divine connection with God. We sense his distress in Psalm 51 at the very thought of his connection being short-circuited or severed. His endeavor to honor his covenant with God required him on many occasions to re-connect to God because he was well aware of the consequences of being disconnected from God.

In God's eyes, these two relationships have great significance in the grand scheme of things…

> **"This is a record of the ancestors of Jesus the Messiah, a descendant of David and of Abraham."**
>
> Matthew 1:1 NLT

Even as we consider the lives of Abraham and David, it is evident that in spite of the many occasions that caused their connection to be short-circuited or severed, they still lived life by divine design because they always made sure to re-connect and re-secure their divine connection to God.

The Master Design: Step One

Right now, you may be that believer who is living in crisis. You may be the one who has lost your joy because your situation seems increasingly overwhelming.

You may have lost all hope because it feels like the depth of the hole that you are in is becoming terrifyingly deeper…so much so that you can't even see the light of day. As you contemplate the dire straits of this current economy, the title of this book may seem like MISSION: *Impossible*!

Be encouraged!! Jesus, the Divine Vine of Love, is the Light of the world that shines through this darkness (John 1:5). *In Christ*, there is no darkness at all (1 John 1:5). This economy might be slack, but in this Light, there is no lack! This economy might be slow, but in this Light, there is "overflow"! His Light radiates joy in sorrow and hope for all of our tomorrows.

A songwriter once wrote, *"Behind every dark cloud, there's a silver lining."* We've become so accustomed to looking at what we see in the world and allowing it to dictate what we believe that we can't see past the dark cloud. It's time we began looking past the dark cloud – what we see in the world and see the silver lining – what's been said in the Word.

As believers, we have an extraordinary advantage over nonbelievers – we have two sets of eyes. We have the ability to see what we see but we also have the ability to see beyond what we see…because there *is* more to this than meets the eye.

For so long, we have been looking at the current state of affairs in the world through our natural eyes…only.

With our natural eyes, we look around and see the disorder and confusion in this world – life-threatening sickness and disease, extreme poverty and lack, excessive drug and alcohol abuse, dissolving marriages and disobedient children, fluctuating food and gas prices, major companies closing, unemployment rising, stock prices diving, wars and rumors of wars.

Discouragement and depression sets in causing us to question our faith in the faithfulness of our faithful Father and His immeasurable love for us.

As a result of being disconnected, natural eyes only see problems.

With our spiritual eyes, we can look into God's Word for light to direct our path as we walk through this dark valley of economic instability. For every problem we face in this life, God has made a promise in His Word that is linked to the principle of faith that leads to our provision.

Before there was ever one problem, His Word was the Solution. Before there was ever one question, His Word was the Answer.

Divine connection enables spiritual eyes to see solutions.

So while the rest of the world is looking around through natural eyes, the Royal Family of God should be looking up through spiritual eyes for solutions to our situations (Psalm 121:1-2).

> **"Blessed are those who trust in the LORD and have made the LORD their hope and confidence."**
>
> **Jeremiah 17:7 NLT**

Hope in the Word brings hopefulness.

We can fully expect to run into resistance while implementing this "Master Plan" because the last thing the enemy wants is for believers to have hope in God.

Hope in God will never disappoint us or make us ashamed. When we trust God, our Source of hope, He will fill us completely with joy and peace so that we will "overflow" with confident hope through the power of the Holy Spirit (Romans 15:13 NLT). Divine connection is what enables us to keep our HOPES up to "**H**old **O**n **P**ersistently **E**xpecting **S**uccess!"

We can fully expect to run into resistance while implementing this "Master Plan" because the last thing the enemy needs is for believers to be convicted about correcting any wrong in our life.

Divine connection comes through divine correction; divine correction comes through divine conviction.

Conviction will come gradually as we master our minds through the Word of God. As the seed of God's Word takes root in our heart, it works to remove the deviant seed of thought planted by the enemy long ago. As the seed of God's Word begins to evolve in our spirit, it will permeate, purge and purify our thoughts. This correction fine-tunes our reception and clears the path for connection with the Divine Vine of Love.

Now is the time for the Royal Family of God to stop living in crisis and start living *in Christ*. Now is the time for the Royal Family of God to stop living life by default and start living life by divine design.

Now is the time for the Royal Family of God to displace the "business as usual" mentality and replace it with "unusual Kingdom business" reality.

WE have to take personal responsibility for the way we govern our lives. WE have to take this first step to master our mind to believe that God's Word is absolutely true…for us…in this day and age.

If we continue to think the way we've been thinking, we'll keep doing what we've been doing the way we've been doing it. If we keep doing what we've been doing the way we've been doing it, we're going to keep getting what we've been getting.

What are you thinking?
What are you doing?
What have you got?

There is much more to our Christian lifestyle than going to church every week. If going to church every week was all it took to experience life by God's divine design, every church-going member in the body of Christ would be living the life.

The much more involves making it our number one priority to master our mind to the wisdom of God until we begin to think like God wants us to think so we can do what God wants us to do so we can get what God wants us to have.

If you are that believer living life by default, in crisis, check your connection…then correct your connection.

If your connection is severed…

Get Connected!

If your connection is short-circuited…

Get Securely Connected!

If you are that believer that is living life by design, *in Christ*, double check your connection.

If your connection is sound…

Stay Securely Connected!

Staying securely connected to the Divine Vine of Love enables us to dispel those deliberate distractions that come to steal our identity, kill our dreams, and destroy our relationships. Divine connection enables us to operate in our destiny of dominion and live life by the divine design God had in mind when He created mankind on this earth…and in the earth made new.

If you don't get anything else from reading this book…

Get Connected!

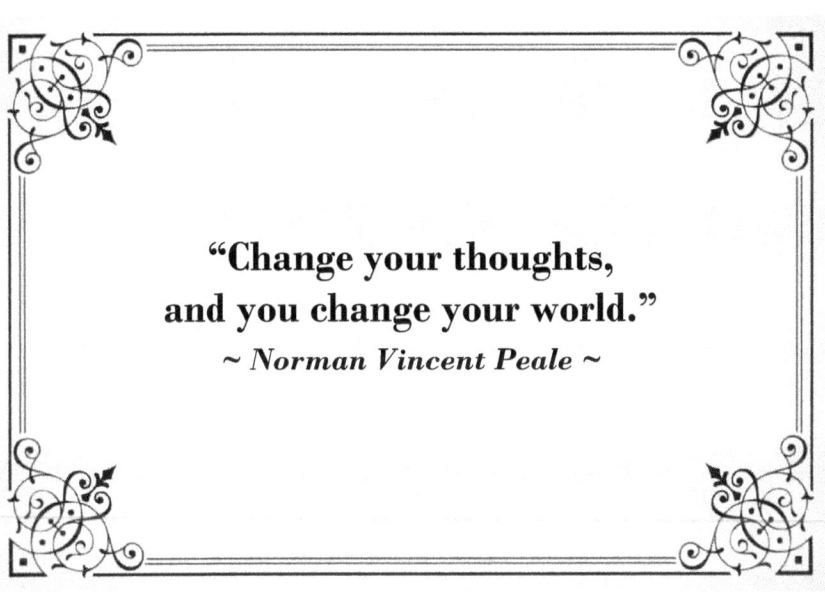

"Change your thoughts,
and you change your world."
~ *Norman Vincent Peale* ~

STEP TWO:
MASTER YOUR MOUTH

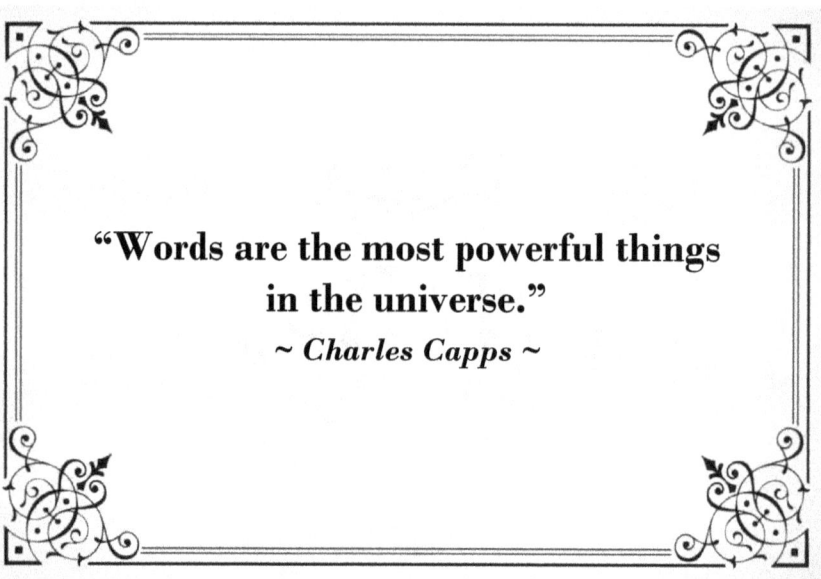

Disturbing Dialect

There is a massive case of murder-suicide occurring right now in the body of Christ. Believers all over the world are literally killing each other and themselves, not with knives and guns…but with words.

"Death and life are in the power of the tongue" is a passage of scripture that is frequently recited with a holy boldness and fervor by many believers. But how many believers really believe the urgent context of Proverbs 18:21? How many believers really believe that death and life are in the power of our tongue? How many believers fully comprehend the magnitude of this passage of scripture?

I suspect what most believers believe is that Proverbs 18:21 ends where *their* recitation of Proverbs 18:21 ends.

It does not.

It continues on to say, *"…they that love it shall eat the fruit thereof."* I love how the *Message Bible* interprets Proverbs 18:21…

> **"Words kill, words give life; they're either poison or fruit – *you choose.*"**

The Choice Is Ours!

Freedom of choice is an awesome privilege that God has gifted us. He has given *us* the power to choose whether we live or whether we die, whether we live blessed or whether we live cursed.

> "Today *I have given you the choice* between life and death, between blessings and curses. Now I call on heaven and earth to witness *the choice you make.* Oh, that you would *choose life,* so that you and your descendants might live!"
>
> **Deuteronomy 30:19 NLT**

We make that choice by the words we speak. We can choose to speak life or we can choose to speak death. Whatever words we choose to speak have consequences that we must be satisfied with – whether good or bad.

Proverbs 18:20 (AMP) confirms it…

> "A man's [moral] self shall be filled with *the fruit of his mouth*; and with the consequence of his words he must be satisfied [whether good or evil]."

Gives a whole new meaning to the expression *"eating your words"*, doesn't it?

If we are not satisfied with the consequences that have resulted from our choice of words, we can change our circumstances by changing our choice of words.

Let the people of God say…

"I Choose To Speak Life!"

Choosing to speak words of life not only saves our life, it saves the lives of our children!

As Christians, we are called "believers" because our calling is to *believe God*. If we profess to believe God, the words we speak should be words of life that lead to a life lived by God's divine design.

Unfortunately, if you listen to the conversation of many Christians who profess to believe God, you will find that far more believers have chosen to speak words of death that have led them to a life lived by default – accepting life "as is" until we all get to heaven.

One of the first spiritual laws established by God in the first chapter of Genesis was the law of seedtime and harvest. The law of seedtime and harvest says that everything produces after its own kind – including our words. Immediately after the flood, God decreed…

> **"As long as the earth endures, *seedtime and harvest*, cold and heat, summer and winter, day and night *will never cease*."**
> **Genesis 8:22 NIV**

Paul affirms the continuity of this law from the Old Testament to the New Testament.

> **"Do not be deceived: God cannot be mocked. *A man reaps what he sows*."**
> **Galatians 6:7 NIV**

The law of seedtime and harvest remains in full effect today, operating with the same precision and power as when God first instituted it. Whether we choose to speak life or death, the law will work for us. The law works however *we* work the law. Of course, it's much more favorable when we choose to speak life.

Naturally speaking, a farmer who sows apple seeds doesn't expect to reap a harvest of oranges; or if he sows kernels of corn, he doesn't expect to see a pod of peas.

Spiritually speaking, believers who sow seeds (words) of death shouldn't expect to reap a life lived by God's divine design; if they sow fear-based words, they shouldn't expect to reap the faith-filled promises of God in their life.

Make no mistake about it, Satan knows the potency of the law of seedtime and harvest because he had a close encounter with Jesus, the incorruptible Seed Who was sown by God to reap a harvest of lost souls.

Satan knows that there is soon coming a time when earth's crop will be fully ripe and the Son of Man will swing His sharp sickle and reap the harvest of saved souls.

Satan is a shrewd dude. He knows that God's Word is a force to be reckoned with. He knows that God's Word spoken in faith from the mouth of a *believing believer* is sharp enough to slice and dice right through his kingdom because God's Word already has...

> **"...he disarmed the spiritual rulers and authorities. He shamed them publicly by his victory over them on the cross."**
>
> **Colossians 2:15 NLT**

Armed with the knowledge that the law of seedtime and harvest works hand in glove with the law of the power of the tongue, Satan has cleverly laced our common communication with what's been deemed credible catchphrases and chichi clichés that are, in actuality, carcinogenic to the health and development of our Inside Man. These catchphrases and clichés are cunningly crafted to obstruct the progression of our spiritual health and development.

It is no coincidence that the memorable recitation – *"sticks and stones may break my bones but words will never hurt me"* was introduced and integrated into our childhood conversation. Our mind and spirit are very impressionable during our formative years. This subtle implant has had a tremendous, devastating ripple effect that has left an adverse imprint on our adult life.

The Master Design: Step Two

If I were to assemble a focus group of men and women right now to discuss how words spoken to them during their formative years have impacted their life, the preposterous presumption that our words have no power to do as much damage as sticks and stones would...

> *Visible physical wounds soon heal;*
> *Invisible emotional wounds, lives steal.*

POOF...be gone.

Not only is this seemingly harmless expression the biggest lie straight from the deepest pits of hell, it is in blatant opposition to the urgent message of Proverbs 18:21.

Having planted this suggestive seed that the words we speak are powerless in our mind, daily Satan works passionately and purposefully to water that seed so that it roots deeply and swells up in our spirit. Deviously, he works to keep us using our words to destroy not only our lives but the lives of others. Diligently, he works to keep us using our words to talk ourselves out of the promises God has *already* blessed us with *in Christ*.

Believers are so adapted to the world's fear-based speaking pattern that we speak fear-filled words instinctively without seriously taking into account the end-product of our words.

Paul warned us in Romans 12:2 (MSG)...

"Don't become so well-adjusted to your culture that you fit into it without even thinking."

Knowing that life and death are in the power of our tongue, shouldn't we pay closer attention to the words that roll off our tongue? Shouldn't we make a conscious effort to choose to speak more words of life than words of death?

For the past year or so, I've been "ear-hustling". I have become increasingly observant of the content of my own conversation as well as other people's conversations – believers and nonbelievers. Not only has my suspicion been confirmed, my questions have been answered.

Most believers *do not* really believe the urgent context of Proverbs 18:21 – that death and life are in the power of our tongue neither do we fully comprehend the magnitude of this passage of scripture.

Look, if we *truly* believed that every word that rolls off our tongue comes to pass in our life, we wouldn't be saying a whole lot of the stuff that we've been saying! If we fully comprehended the magnitude of this passage of scripture, we would roll up our tongue until we mastered our mouth to speak spirit-filled words of life.

The truth is *every* word that rolls off our tongue comes to pass in our life – sooner or later – in some shape, form or fashion. Our life today is a full-blown exposition of words we've spoken or words we've allowed to be spoken over our life.

Earlier we determined that sometimes a delay in manifestation can be traced back to a delinquency in application. But sometimes a delay in manifestation can be traced back to our selection of words.

As believers, our words should always line up with God's Word and our actions should always line up with our words. Our actions should not be negated by our words; our actions should be dictated by our words. In other words, we should not say one thing and do another; we should do what we say.

Our actions are expressions of our expectations. When we expect what we say to come to pass, we act like we expect what we say will come to pass. The problem is most believers say one thing and do another because they're expectations are slim to none – they don't really expect what they say to come to pass in their life…but it always does.

Jesus says in Mark 11:23 that *we can have what we say*. Therefore, we should expect what we say to come to pass in our life...especially when we're speaking God's Word over our life.

God's Word always performs...

> **"The rain and snow come down from the heavens and stay on the ground to water the earth. They cause the grain to grow, producing seed for the farmer and bread for the hungry. It is the same with my word. I send it out, and *it always produces fruit. It will accomplish all I want it to, and it will prosper everywhere I send it.*"**
>
> **Isaiah 55:10-11 NLT**

In the beginning, God saw what He said because He expected to see what He said. His actions lined up with His words. He expected to see light when He ordered light to be. He expected the sun to shine during the day and the moon at night when He ordered the day to be divided from the night. God saw what He said because He expected to see what He said.

As God's "mini-me's", we should mimic His actions. We should say what we want to see in our life (what the Word says we should have in our life) – expect to see what we say come to pass in our life and act like we expect what we've said has come to pass in our life. We need to raise our expectations because...

Divine Intervention responds to Divine Expectation.

This character flaw – our proficiency at saying one thing and doing another – affects every area of our life. It is not specific to just our spiritual selves.

One prime example in the physical realm of this teeter-totter mentality is the challenge of weight loss.

With the epidemic of obesity sweeping the nation, it's not difficult to find at least one somebody (and that somebody could be us) who at the beginning of every year or every month or every week or even every day, who promises to eat less and exercise more so they can lose 25 pounds, 45 inches, two dress sizes and one shoe size.

What usually happens is they end up eating more and exercising less (if at all) and either losing no weight or gaining even more.

Another prime example is in the area of finances. We promise to spend less and save more and you guessed it, at the end of the day, we spend more and save nothing!

We all talk a good game but when the rubber meets the road, the truth will be told.

It's one thing for believers to talk the talk (and believe me, there are a bunch of believers bumping their gums about how they *believe God*) but a genuine spirit of faith not only talks the talk, a genuine spirit of faith walks the walk...even when it's not comfortable or convenient.

God knows the unruly nature of our tongue all too well. In His infinite wisdom, God has implemented restrictions when it comes to our deviant tongue and His divine timing.

You might be thinking, *"Well, why would He do that? I thought it was His will that I experience His promises in my life."*

That's exactly WHY He did that.

Just imagine for one moment what would happen if God removed those restrictions for twenty-four hours – if God granted us instant gratification and declared that every word we spoke, within that 24-hour period, would come to pass in our life...instantly.

Right about now, somebody might be shouting, *"YES, LORD, DO IT!"* But before you get too happy or shout too hard, realize this...unless your mind has been renewed by the Word of God and your mouth has been refined by the Spirit of God, you are highly likely to *say something* during the course of that 24-hour period that will put you six feet under. You may start out good being careful to watch what you say but I promise you that at some point during those twenty-four hours, you will slip up and say something that will kill you dead.

If God removed those restraints for twenty-four hours, funeral directors across the globe would be inundated with business as millions of believers would drop dead on the spot…because of their *choice of words*!

It may sound radical…but guess what? It's radically real.

Now being the "saved, sanctified, Holy Ghost-filled, fire-baptized, Jesus on your side and running for your life" saint that you are, you personally may not have uttered any of the following credible catchphrases and chichi clichés on my list. You may be one of the ones who *really* believes the urgent context and fully comprehends the magnitude of Proverbs 18:21. However, you may know somebody who has said one or two of these phrases or maybe you've heard them…in passing.

Take a minute to peruse this list of catchphrases and clichés. Trust me, by the time you get to the end of this list almost every one of these statements will be checked off and you might have even more to add.

As you read them, keep in mind two things: 1) death and life are in the power of our tongue and 2) you can have what you say.

At the very top of this list is perhaps the most widely used "credible" catchphrase…

I love you to death…

When you really stop and think about this cliché, you will realize it's an oxymoron! Loving someone to death is what can be dubbed by another catchphrase – "cruel kindness".

Personally, I've stopped committing suicide and have stopped allowing my family members, friends and acquaintances to commit "murder in the first" on my life. I don't ever allow people who say they love me to tell me that they *"love me to death"*. If my family and friends really love me, they must *"love me to life"*.

Sounds strange, right? Why does loving someone *"to life"* sound strange but loving someone *"to death"* sound okay?

Pencils ready?

She talked me to death...
I'm freezing to death...
You scared me to death...
He bored me to death...
This thing will be the death of me...
My child is worrying me to death...
That just tickled me to death...
I died laughing...
I'm dead serious...
I was dead silent...
I am dead tired...
She was dead sleep...
I am sick and tired...
My head is killing me...
My tooth is killing me...
My feet are killing me...
My stomach is killing me...
My sinuses are killing me...
My back is killing me...
My kids are killing me...
My job is killing me...

The Master Design: Step Two

What kills me is…
I was killing myself…
It just kills me when…
It was killing me not to…
It will kill me if I have to…
You're killing me, dude…
The suspense is killing me…
They would kill me if they found out…
I'm just killing time…
I am dressed to kill…
She killed that song…
We're going to make a killing…
I'll do it this way until the day I die…
I'd rather die before I do that…
When I heard that, I thought I'd just die…
It was to die for…
I was about to die…
I almost died when…
I was dying when…
I was dying of thirst…
I'm dying to go…
I'm dying to know…
I'm dying to see it…
If I'm lying, I'm dying…
I'm going to die if I don't…
We were dying to…
You'll do it over my dead body…

I thought I'd died and gone to heaven…
You are dead wrong…
He is such a deadbeat…
You are dead meat…
She must be brain dead…
You're a dead duck…
That was a death trap…
It's do or die…
Get rich or die trying…
I'm afraid I can't go…
I'm afraid I don't have…
Well I'll be damned…
God damn you…
Drop dead…
He was standing at death's door…
Cross my heart and hope to die…
I'm serious as a heart attack…
I'm about to go crazy…
They were driving me crazy…
I think I'm going out of my mind…
My husband is about to make me lose my mind…
My kids are going to drive me insane…

What about this chichi cliché that has attained major popularity in the church coming straight out of the pulpit right into the pews?

Somebody ought to praise God like
you're about to lose your mind up in here!

MY…MY…MY!

When are we going to get it, people? Satan wants our minds. He knows the potent power of a sound mind that trusts God in the midst of the most challenging circumstances. He knows that the way to our mind is through our mouth. He knows that the way to get to our mouth is through our mind.

> *Our thoughts become words and our words feed our thoughts.*

He knows the potency of the mind-mouth connection. That's why he's programmed us to speak these "death sentences" into our lives and the lives of others on a daily basis.

I'm sure *you've* been delivered from speaking these death sentences but maybe you know some folk who have not been delivered and speak death wishes on a regular basis over their own life...and yours!

I have a girlfriend who would start every story she was about to tell me with *"You're just gonna die when I tell you this"* or *"It's gonna kill you when I tell you..."* At first, even though it bothered me a *tiny wee bit*, I didn't bother to say anything because I knew she didn't really think I was going to die or that it would kill me when she told me the story. She was just using common clichés people often use when communicating.

Well, that's *exactly* what the devil wanted. He wanted me to think nothing of it and just let her continue to say what she'd been saying.

Oh but when I came to myself and realized that Proverbs 18:21 is a Universal Law and that I was *allowing* her to use the power in her tongue to speak death into *my* life...

Let the people of God say...

"GOD ALLOWS WHAT WE ALLOW."

From that point on, when she would preface her stories with these clichés, I would politely reply, *"Then don't tell me"* or *"No, I'm not going to die"* or *"No, it's not going to kill me"*. As time passed, she became more mindful of using those phrases when speaking to me. Now I don't know what she does when she's talking to anybody else but I do know that she makes a conscious effort not to say those things to me.

What's funny is, if other people say these catchphrases or clichés to me in her presence, she'll look at me and say to them, *"Don't say that to her!"*

These are just a few of many "harmless" catchphrases and clichés that are quite often recited with no *real thought* given to the consequence of certain destruction. Why? Because our mindsets are wrapped so tightly around operating in this type of demented demeanor that we are oblivious to the damages.

The argument most people make when they use these catchphrases and clichés is *"Well, you know what I mean."* Clearly, the same way people say one thing and do something else people say one thing and mean something else.

That's probably one reason so many believers are sitting in the waiting room waiting for God to say or do or give them *something else*. They know what God has said but what they think is *"Well, certainly God must mean something else"* or *"Surely God is going to do something else."*

God doesn't do what we do. He says what He means and He means what He says. He's already done what He said He would do and He did it well. God expects us to do what *He* does…not vice versa.

He is the Master-Me;
We are the mini-me's.

In my mind, I knew that my girlfriend wasn't intentionally trying to kill me when she would say what she said (or at least I hope she wasn't. ☺) She was simply saying one thing and meaning something else. BUT...as far as my spirit was concerned, she meant exactly what she said.

Our spirit doesn't interpret; it facilitates. Rather than translate the words it records, our spirit seeks to transfer those recorded words into our life. It doesn't decipher what was said to mean something else other than what was said. It doesn't read between the lines. It doesn't read the fine print. It doesn't analyze the tone or spirit in which it was said. When it comes to our spirit, what you *say* is what you get.

Let the people of God say...

"IT IS WHAT IT IS."

Not only do we puzzle people when we don't say what we mean, more importantly, we perplex our spirits and most importantly, it piques God.

This type of behavior is double-mindedness at its best. This type of behavior is how Satan keeps believers conformed to the world.

The Word tells us that a double-minded man is...

> "...unstable and unreliable and uncertain about everything [he thinks, feels, decides]".
>
> **James 1:8 AMP**

God has not given us a double-mind; He's given us a sound mind – a mind that is free from moral defects and exercises good judgment. True to Satan's strategy to pervert God's precepts, the attributes of a double-mind are directly contrary to the attributes of a sound mind.

So many believers are living unstable lives because they have allowed their spirits to receive unreliable, mixed messages. As a result, they are uncertain about everything in their life.

This is a serious issue. Believers who waver like the waves of the sea – going up and down, back and forth, side to side – will not receive anything they ask for from the Lord.

Listen, all day every day, we are either speaking words of life or we are speaking words of death. Our words are either beneficial to us or detrimental to us – they are either productive or destructive. Our words are either encouraging us or encumbering us. Our words are either blessing us or cursing us.

There is no in-between; no gray area. Our words either have a positive effect or a negative effect on our life.

When we choose to speak words of life, the Light of God's glory shines brightly in us and on us and our life experience will be a reflection of God's divine design for us.

When we choose to speak words of death, the Light goes out and our life experience will be dark and dismal.

People of God, if we are to walk in our destiny of dominion and live life by God's divine design – an abundant life of power, peace and prosperity – we need to master our mind to habitually *think God's thoughts* so we can master our mouth to habitually *speak God's words* and habitually *do God's will* until our character reflects *His character*.

As we allow the Spirit of God to renew our mind through the Word of God, we must also allow the Spirit of God to refine our mouth to speak the Word of God because, as it stands, our current disturbing dialect is literally a matter of life and death and…

BELIEVERS NEED TO BELIEVE THAT!

DIVINE AMMUNITION

Believers may not really believe the urgent context or fully comprehend the magnitude of Proverbs 18:21, but be very sure that Satan really believes and fully comprehends it. He knows for a certainty that our faith-filled words are divine ammunition in this spiritual warfare against him and all the forces of evil in his kingdom of darkness. God's Word spoken in faith out of the mouth of a born-again Spirit-filled believer is Satan's second worst nightmare.

Our words are much more powerful than we've been led to believe. Our words have the power to make us sick or well; the power to make us rich or poor; the power to make us fat or skinny; the power to keep our families together or tear them apart; the power to find us employment or keep us unemployed; the power to detain us or deliver us; the power to save us or sink us.

Yes, sticks and stones may break our bones but you had better believe that words have the power to hurt…or help us.

Let the people of God say…

"I'VE GOT THE POWER!"

Our belief system is contaminated because our thoughts have been programmed by the culture of this world. If our contaminated belief system is ever to be cleansed and changed, it must be washed with water through the Word.

In His parable of the wise and foolish builders, Jesus uses the fundamental principles of construction to articulate the importance of making God's Word *the* number one priority in our life.

> "These words I speak to you are not incidental additions to your life, homeowner improvements to your standard of living. *They are foundational words, words to build a life on.* If you work these words into your life, you are like a smart carpenter who built his house on solid rock. Rain poured down, the river flooded, a tornado hit—but nothing moved that house. It was fixed to the rock.
>
> "But if you just use my words in Bible studies and *don't work them into your life*, you are like a stupid carpenter who built his house on the sandy beach. When a storm rolled in and the waves came up, it collapsed like a house of cards."
>
> Matthew 7:24-27 MSG

Many believers today have chosen to build their life on the shallow, shaky foundation of this world and not on the solid, sure foundation of the Word. Now during this economic earthquake, they are visibly shaken as the pressure presses in and their lives begin to collapse like a house of cards. As a last resort, they run to God sobbin' and spittin' and slobbin' and snottin' asking *"Why me, Lord, why me?"*

In Luke's account of this same parable of the wise and foolish builders in chapter 6 verse 46 (NLT), Jesus asks...

> "So why do you keep calling me 'Lord, Lord!' *when you don't do what I say?*"

Jesus' instruction – *"work these words into your life"* in Matthew 7:25 echoes God's instruction in Joshua 1:8 – *"meditate therein day and night, that thou mayest observe to do according to all that is written therein"*.

People of God, I want you to be very clear about this...

GOD'S WORD ALWAYS WORKS.

The Word will do the work in our life when we work the Word into our life.

The Word will do the work in our life when we make the Word our *first choice*...not our last resort.

> **"Seek the Kingdom of God *above all else*, and live righteously, and he will give you everything you need."**
>
> **Matthew 6:33 NLT**

God is very clear in His instructions about how believers are to live life by divine design on this earth. Sadly, like the children of Israel, the body of Christ doesn't want to follow **ALL** of His instructions. We want to do what *we* want to do, *when* we want to do it, *how* we want to do it...BUT we want to achieve the same results.

We want to seek God only when we need God. We want to seek God only when it's convenient for us. We want to live our life (like it's our life to live) how we want to live our life *and still expect* to reap the rewards of those who diligently seek Him.

Let the people of God say...

"THAT'S NOT QUITE HOW IT WORKS."

True, God has gifted us with the freedom of choice but He also advises us to *"choose life, so that you and your descendants might live"*.

I love what Joyce Meyer says about this verse. She says (and I paraphrase) that Deuteronomy 30:19 is like a multiple choice test.

 a. choose life
 b. choose death
 c. **choose a**

If God tells us to do *this* and *that*, we can't choose to do *this* and not *that* and expect God to do what He would do if we did this *and* that.

If we desire to live life by God's divine design in this life...on this earth, we *must* work God's Word into our life and follow **ALL** of His instructions.

The efficacy of our divine ammunition is totally dependant on our ultimate obedience to God's divine decrees.

We cannot and will not be able to demolish the vice-like grip the enemy has on our life using the words the world speaks. Those are *his* words that he has designed to work *for him* and *against us*.

2 Corinthians 10:4 (NIV) tells us that the weapons we fight with are not the weapons of the world. On the contrary, our divine ammunition, the sword of the Spirit – the Word of God, has divine power to demolish demonic strongholds.

Disconnection from the world and reconnection with the Word is the order of the day. If we are to walk in our destiny of dominion and live life by God's divine design, we must adamantly reject the world's way of doing things and attentively respect the Word's way of doing things.

The world's system is designed and destined to fail…and is failing. Why? It has been erected and established on a feeble foundation of fear and greed.

The Word system is designed and destined to flourish…and is flourishing. Why? It has been erected and established on a firm Foundation of faith and grace.

Working God's Word into our life begins with believing God's Word in our heart then speaking God's Word over our life.

That's why Step One: Master Your Mind is a critical, foundational step. We'll never be able to express the Word of God with our mouth if we don't embed the Word of God in our heart.

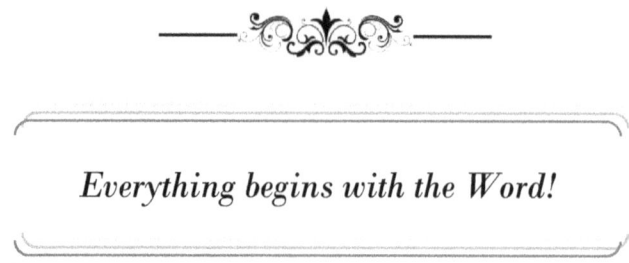

Everything begins with the Word!

God is a "Speaking Spirit" Who created the heaven and the earth in the beginning…*with His words*.

In Genesis 1:2, we find the Spirit of God brooding over the darkness that covered the empty, formless surface of the watery deep. There are many interesting points to note about this one passage of scripture but the point I'd like to make is although the Spirit of God was present in the midst of this dark, dismal watery deep, He did not use His presence to dominate the darkness, He used His words.

> **"*And God said*, Let there be light: and there was light."**

The fact that the very first recorded spoken words of God were used to dominate darkness is of monumental significance. Remember, the *"Law of First Mention"* or the *"Divine Law of Firsts"* states that the first mention of a subject in the Word has special significance because it establishes an *unchangeable pattern* and *sets the stage* for how that subject is to be understood throughout the Word.

In the beginning, God established an unchangeable pattern that set the stage for how He intended for us to use our words when He commanded the light to shine out of darkness.

This first occurrence of light being used to dominate darkness set the stage for the last occurrence of Light being used to dominate darkness.

> **"I have come as a light to shine in this dark world, so that all who put their trust in me will no longer remain in the dark."**
>
> **John 12:46 NLT**

God used His Word – Jesus, the Light of the world – to dominate this kingdom of darkness. His Word became flesh to destroy the works of the devil and to deliver us *from* the dominion of darkness and deliver us *to* our destiny of dominion in the Kingdom of Love.

> **"THEREFORE BE imitators of God [*copy Him and follow His example*], as well-beloved children [imitate their father]."**
>
> **Ephesians 5:1 AMP**

We are created with God's DNA – God's **D**ivine **N**ature and **A**ppearance. As such, we too are speaking spirits with the same ability to use words – God's Words – spoken in faith from our mouth to dominate the darkness in our life and in our world.

God used His Words as divine ammunition and provided us with this same divine arsenal of lethal weapons which we can choose to use or abuse. It is not only our destiny but our privilege to use His Word as divine ammunition. We have been given this divine ammunition to demolish the giants in our life, to dominate the evil forces over our life and designate the promises of God into our life.

It is our responsibility to faithfully speak His Word over our life until it becomes flesh – *takes form*, dwells – *takes residence* in our life and destroys – *takes authority* over the works of the devil.

In six words in three locations, God gives specific instructions about how believers are to live life by His divine design on this earth.

Let the people of God say...

"THE JUST SHALL LIVE BY FAITH."

Romans 1:17; Galatians 3:11; Hebrews 10:38

There are two primary reasons every believer should be living a life of faith.

1. To comply with God's directive;
2. To conform to God's objective.

2 Corinthians 5:7 (AMP) says...

> **"For we walk by faith [*we regulate our lives and conduct ourselves by our conviction or belief respecting man's relationship to God* and divine things, with trust and holy fervor; thus we walk] not by sight or appearance."**

God's *directive* for His people is that we recalibrate our lives and learn to lean on Him and trust in Him with complete confidence simply because He said so and because we know He can be trusted.

> **"Trust in the LORD with all thine heart; and lean not unto thine own understanding. In all thy ways acknowledge him, and he shall direct thy paths."**
>
> **Proverbs 3:5-6**

God's *objective* for us is to stay divinely connected to Him so our lives can be transformed and our image will be conformed to the image of His Son so that the Word can perform with precision and power in our life.

> **"I am the vine; you are the branches. If a man remains in me and I in him, he will bear much fruit; *apart from me you can do nothing.*"**
>
> **John 15:5 NIV**

When an individual makes the choice to live life as a physician, they must attend medical school to develop their aptitude in the area of medicine.

When an individual makes the choice to live life as an attorney, they must attend law school to develop their capabilities in the area of law.

When an individual makes the choice to live life as a believer, they must attend to the Word of God to develop their capacity in the area of faith and love.

Everything God requires us to do He has already equipped us to do. God requires us to live by faith therefore He's given each of us the measure of faith (Romans 12:3). God requires us to walk in love; therefore He's poured out His love into our hearts by the Holy Spirit (Romans 5:5).

But it is our responsibility to develop the measure of faith He's given us and share the love He's poured into us.

Faith and love are birds of a feather that flock together. Without faith, it is impossible to please God (Hebrews 11:6) and without love...well, faith won't work (Galatians 5:6).

> *Faith and love are joined at the hip!*

Just as most individuals take for granted the importance of developing our physical muscles, most believers take for granted the importance of developing our faith and love muscles.

Although the concept of faith is intangible and mysterious to some, God's Word is very clear about what *faith is, how faith comes* and *how faith operates.*

> **"FAITH IS the confidence that what we hope for will actually happen; it gives us assurance about things we cannot see."**
>
> **Hebrews 11:1 NLT**

Simply put, faith goes beyond knowing that God can or that God will...

> *Faith is knowing that God already has!*

As with Proverbs 18:21, many believers believe that Romans 10:17 ends where *their* recitation ends...

> **"So then FAITH COMETH by hearing..."**

It does not.

It continues on to say *"and hearing by the word of God."* The *New Living Translation* of Romans 10:17 says that faith comes from hearing the Good News about Christ. The word "cometh" in the original *King James,* which is the archaic term for the word "come", is present tense.

If the selected verb tense was past tense, this verse would read "So then *faith came*". If the selected verb tense was future tense, it would read "So then *faith will come*". Instead, it reads in modern day vernacular "So then *faith comes*".

Faith is always "in the now". The *King James Version* of Hebrews 11:1 totally supports this assertion...

> **"NOW FAITH is the substance of things hoped for, the evidence of things not seen."**

Merriam Webster's online dictionary defines the word "now" as *"at the present time or moment."* Faith should be ever present and operational every moment of our life. Our faith should *always* be in high gear.

If we took the liberty to remove the comma between the words "hearing" and "and", this scripture would read – *"faith comes by hearing and hearing by the Word of God"* – implying that **FAITH COMES** by *continually hearing* the Good News about Christ.

> **"It is written: 'I believed; therefore I have spoken.' With that same *spirit of faith* we also believe and therefore speak."**

2 Corinthians 4:13 (NIV) tells us how **FAITH OPERATES**... the spirit of faith *believes and speaks.*

Our new life *in Christ* began by faith. With our heart we *believed* that we were made right with God and with our mouth we *confessed* our belief and were saved (Romans 10:10).

Ephesians 2:8 confirms Romans 10:10 – *"by grace are ye saved through faith"* (through believing and speaking).

The written Word of God (LOGOS) teaches us to "**L**ive **O**ut **G**od's **O**rdinances **S**uccessfully."

When the written Word of God is spoken (RHEMA) over our life, we "**R**elease **H**is **E**xcellent **M**anifestation in **A**bundance" into our life.

This is the common thread weaved through the fabric of Joshua 1:8, Romans 1:17, Romans 10:17, Hebrews 11:1 and 2 Corinthians 4:13…and let's not forget James 1:22 and James 2:26.

The just shall live by continually hearing the good news about Christ and meditating on that Word day and night so that we develop an aggressive spirit of faith that has a rock solid belief in the Word of God, boldly speaks the Word of God and demonstrates corresponding action with the Word.

After reading John Osteen's book, *There is a Miracle in Your Mouth*, which conveys the very essence of the spirit of faith, *"There is a miracle in MY mouth"* became my personal maxim.

I get that the words I speak decide where I abide. If I choose to continue my worldly speech pattern and live my worldly life, my wilderness experience will be my final destination on this earth. If I choose to believe and faithfully speak the Word I've heard over my life, I will experience the life by divine design God has in mind for me.

Even as challenging as my circumstances appear at times or as stifling as my situations feel, I try hard not to say what I feel like saying (although sometimes I am moved by my emotions); instead I say what I *need to* say.

What I *need* to say is what *God says*. As nonsensical or supernatural as this may sound to some, it is most certainly sound to me.

I speak life to every dead situation in my life – whether it's in my family, in my finances, in my body, in my mind – whatever it is, however it looks. I don't say what I see at the moment, I say what I want to see in a moment.

> "There's far more here than meets the eye. *The things we see now are here today, gone tomorrow. But the things we can't see now will last forever.*"
>
> 2 Corinthians 4:18 MSG

This mini-me is simply imitating my Heavenly Father, Master-Me (the Master of me)...

> "...Who *gives life to the dead* and speaks of the nonexistent things that [He has foretold and promised] as if they [already] existed."
>
> Romans 4:17 AMP

...because in His mind, they already do exist.

You see, when we master our mind to believe that God has *already* done what He promised, we can master our mouth to speak those promises over our life with authority and audacity. We should always speak the promises God prophesied into our life as if they already exist...because they do already exist.

Faith that knows *God already has* constantly confesses in the present tense. Constantly confessing what *God has already done* will increase our faith because constant confession means continual hearing.

> "I will praise thee for ever, because *thou hast done it*: and I will wait on thy name; for it is good before thy saints."
>
> Psalm 52:9

Instead of always talking about what *God is getting ready to* do, we should be talking about what *God has already done*.

> "*God has already turned my situation around...*
> I AM living His divine design for my life!"

> "*God has already divinely healed my body...*
> I AM walking in divine health and I am whole!"

"God has already restored my marriage…
The glory of this latter house is greater than the former!"

"God has already brought my unruly child back home…
Saved, sanctified, delivered, healed and set free!"

"God has already blessed me with a new job…
I mind my own business and I AM my own boss!"

"God has already gotten me out of debt…
I AM financially free and living prosperously!"

"God has already blessed me with a fine home…
I AM living in a well-furnished house that I did not buy!"

"God has already blessed me with a new car…
Cash & Carry!"

"God has already done everything He promised He'd do in my life…
I AM living an abundant life of power, peace & prosperity."

It's a virtual circle because the more we believe, the more we speak; the more we speak, the more we hear; the more we hear, the more we believe and the more we speak…thus the circle remains unbroken.

The only way to prohibit the enemy from prevailing in preventing the promises of God from manifesting in our life is to use God's Word as our divine ammunition.

The only way to invoke the supernatural power that brings life to every dead situation and demolishes every demonic stronghold in our life is to use our divine ammunition.

You may or may not believe you have any demonic strongholds in your life but know that the reason we are not living out our destiny of dominion is due to a diabolical force that seeks to usurp our authority.

You may or may not believe you have any dead situations in your life but know that every situation in our life that is not in line with the divine design God has in mind for our life is a dead situation.

All during His earthly ministry, Jesus spoke life over every dead – spiritual and natural – situation that He faced because as He told His disciples in John 6:63 (MSG)...

> **"Every word I've spoken to you is a Spirit-word, and so *it is life-making*."**

Jesus' words were Spirit-filled and life-making because He said exactly what His Father, the Spirit Who created all life, taught Him to say (John 8:28).

As speaking spirits, we *should* imitate our Brother who imitated our Father and only speak Spirit-filled, life-making words over our life and the lives of others.

But because our thinking has been programmed by the culture of this world, our speech is patterned after the culture of this world and instead of using *His words* to work for us we've been using our words against ourselves.

We spend way too much time speaking destructive catchphrases and clichés. We spend so much time "speaking of the devil" and how busy he is that we don't even have much time left to talk about *how good God is*.

Let the people of God say...

"GOD IS STILL GOOD AND I AM STILL GOD'S ...SO IT'S ALL GOOD!"

God gave us power over **ALL** the power of the enemy. We either invoke or revoke that power by the words we speak. The more time we spend talking about how busy the devil is, the more we revoke our power and pass our baton of dominion to him.

The more time we spend talking about the goodness of God, the more we invoke our power and activate our destiny of dominion over the enemy.

The Psalmist said it best in Psalm 34:1...

> **"I will bless the LORD at all times:** *his praise shall continually* **be in my mouth."**

The Apostle Paul concurs with King David's declaration of adoration.

> **"Therefore, let us offer through Jesus** *a continual sacrifice of praise to God,* **proclaiming our allegiance to his name."**
>
> **Hebrews 13:15 NLT**

A songwriter posed this question...

"Who's on the Lord's side?"

A commercial proposed this answer...

"Raise your hand...if you're sure."

Are we positively certain of our allegiance to God and Kingdom business? If we are, the fruit of our lips should always be praising and promoting God's Best...not Satan's mess.

As ambassadors – highly-esteemed, authorized representatives of Christ sent by the government of God to represent the Kingdom of God during our temporary mission here on earth – our life should be a reflection of our representation. Our life is a literal walking billboard and our words determine what's posted on the billboard.

In his classic book, *The Tongue: A Creative Force*, Charles Capps says Jesus revealed to him, *"I have told My people they can have what they say, but My people are saying what they have."*

We won't change what we're seeing in our life until we change what we're saying about our life. The world tells us that *"what we see is what we get"* but the Word tells us *"what we say is what we get"*!

But again, we can't change what we're saying about our life until we change what we are "seeing" in our life.

Our thoughts are our mind's eye. Our words project our thoughts into our life. If in our mind's eye we "see" ourselves sick, we will speak about how sick we are.

> *"It feels like I'm coming down with the flu.*
> *It never fails when flu season comes around*
> *I always get bitten by the bug."*

Well, guess what? Every time the flu season comes around, you will get bitten by the bug.

If in our mind's eye we "see" ourselves broke, we will speak about how broke we are.

> *"I guess I'll be robbing Peter and Paul*
> *to pay Mary again this paycheck."*

Well, guess what? When pay day comes, Peter and Paul are going to get robbed and Mary is going to get paid.

Because we live in the negative flow of this world, instinctively we gravitate toward the negative before we even contemplate the positive.

> *"I just know something is going to happen at the last*
> *minute and I'll be late for my appointment."*
>
> *"I bet you my last dollar that one of my kids will get*
> *sick right before we go on vacation."*

What we "see" in our mind's eye affects what we say out of our mouth and what we say out of our mouth affects what we see in our life.

Every day our mind writes, directs and produces mental motion pictures. Generally, most people are "seeing" negative footage in their mind's eye. So naturally, what's coming out of their mouth is a negative soundtrack. Ultimately, most people's lives are a full-length production of this negative footage and soundtrack.

If every day all we talk about are all the problems we're facing, all the pain we're feeling, all the bills we're paying, we will remain imprisoned in our circumstantial cell block.

If, however, every day, all we talk about are all the ways God has blessed us exceedingly, healed us completely, and provided for us sufficiently, there will be a prison break.

The more we say what we see, the more we'll see what we're saying – whether good, bad or indifferent.

Why? Because Jesus says *we can have what we say*!

Our speech can only be corrected when our heart is *securely* connected. The words of our mouth will only be acceptable in God's sight when the meditations of our heart align with His Word.

Remember what Jesus said...

> **"These words I speak to you are not incidental additions to your life; homeowner improvements to *your standard of living.*"**
>
> **Matthew 7:24 MSG**

They are not words to work around our life; they are words that we must work into our life. They are not words that line up with our lifestyle; our lifestyle must line up with the Word. They are words to build our life on.

As in construction, the stability of any building is determined by the caliber of the foundation the building has been erected upon.

The Master Design: Step Two 139

The foundational principles of Step One are the driving force behind Steps Two and Three. We will never be able to *"Master Our Mouth"* or *"Master Our Money"* if we do not first *"Master Our Mind"*.

It's high time we begin following **ALL** the instructions and start speaking the Word over our life to "fix" our lifestyle, and stop skewing the Word to "fit" our lifestyle.

Ending our recitation at *"faith comes by hearing"* has been detrimental to our spiritual health and development.

Faith in whatever we're hearing comes by hearing it repeatedly. Faith in God's Word comes by hearing God's Word repeatedly. Faith in fear comes by hearing fearful things repeatedly.

When you stop to think about it, though, most "church-goers" do hear God's Word repeatedly. So what's the problem?

The problem is we're hearing God's Word "repeatedly" one or two days of the week but we're repeatedly listening to the "sweet nothings" the enemy whispers in our ear every day of the week. Essentially, most believers are more highly developed in their faith in fear than their faith in God.

The average American spends six hours and 47 minutes each day watching television. According to the Bureau of Labor Statistics "American Time Use Survey" conducted in 2009, *"watching TV was the leisure activity that occupied the most time."*

> *More believers are average Americans than disciplined Disciples.*

Suffice it to say, if we're spending almost one-third of our day feeding nonsense to our spirits – watching nauseating news reports, jam-packed with fear from the top of the hour to the last hurrah, ridiculous reality shows riddled with vile language and "conduct unbecoming", programs focused on paranormal activity, racy music videos tainted with explicit sexual behavior, countless drama-filled court and cop shows, horrifying episodes about hospital traumas, and the list goes on – what the Word said would happen *has* happened.

> **"For people will love only themselves and their money. They will be boastful and proud, scoffing at God, disobedient to their parents, and ungrateful. They will consider nothing sacred. They will be unloving and unforgiving; they will slander others and have no self-control. They will be cruel and hate what is good. They will betray their friends, be reckless, be puffed up with pride, and love pleasure rather than God. They will act religious, but they will reject the power that could make them godly."**
>
> 2 Timothy 3:2-5 NLT

Our society has experienced an extensive ethical decay over the last several decades that has slowly infiltrated the body of Christ.

Repeatedly feasting on this putrid food that has no nutritional value has programmed the minds of believers to have more faith in fearful things than faith in the things of God. Too much television has distorted our vision, bloated us with fear, preoccupied our time and made us too lazy to spend *quality* time in the Word.

There's an old proverb that says, *"An idle mind is the devil's workshop."*

The devil just loves idle minds because he knows that idle minds speak idle words and idle words are insignificant to him because they pose no threat to him.

At first glance, idle words appear innocent and inconsequential.

They are not.

Jesus says in Matthew 12:36 that we will give an account for every idle word we speak. The *Message Bible's* blunt interpretation says…

> **"Let me tell you something: Every one of these careless words is going to come back to haunt you. There will be a time of Reckoning."**

What's more, Jesus says in Luke 12:2-3 (NLT)...

"The time is coming when everything that is covered up will be revealed, and *all that is secret will be made known to all*. Whatever you have said in the dark will be heard in the light, and what you have whispered behind closed doors will be shouted from the housetops for all to hear!"

Let the people of God say...

"Uh-Oh!"

Whether we believe it or not, we give an account for the idle words we speak every day of our life. If we are speaking words that are not producing life and blessings in our life, we are speaking idle – Inoperative, Delusive, Lifeless, Empty – words.

For all you diehard advocates of the evening news, let me ask you this: Is it really necessary for you to know what's going on in the world more than you need to know what's going on in the Word?

Faith in God's Word doesn't come by hearing what's going on in the world. Faith in fear does. Don't you know that you can find out what's going on in the world by reading the Word?

The story is told in Luke 10:38-42 (NIV) of Jesus' visit to the home of Martha and Mary. Martha gladly welcomed Jesus into their home but immediately became *distracted* with everything she had to do to prepare a festive dinner for the Master. Mary, on the other hand, sat attentively at Jesus' feet listening to His Word.

Martha became frustrated by Mary's lack of support and confronted Jesus asking, *"Lord, don't you care that my sister has left me to do the work by myself? Tell her to help me!"*

"Martha, Martha," the Lord answered, "you are worried and upset about many things, *but only one thing is needed*. Mary has chosen what is better, and it will not be taken away from her."

Jesus' response to Martha confirms that Mary's choice was far more important than Martha's choice. Martha chose to hustle and bustle to prepare food for physical nourishment while Mary's choice was quietude and serenity as she received food that would nourish her spirit. Jesus said, *"Mary has chosen what is better…"*

The *Amplified Bible* translation of Romans 10:17 says…

> **"*Faith comes* by hearing [what is told], and what is heard comes by the preaching [of the message that came from the lips] of Christ (the Messiah Himself)."**

This thing is serious. The time is coming soon when our faith in God is going to be **ALL** we have. No preachers, no churches, no services, no bibles; the only thing we will have is our faith in God.

If we don't begin to prepare for that day by following **ALL** the instructions and exercising our faith and love muscles now and continue to stay asleep at the wheel, when that time comes, like the five foolish virgins in the parable found in Matthew 25:1-13, we'll be caught off guard and start trying to do what we *should have been doing all along*…a day late and a dollar short.

Let the people of God say…

"I'M DOING WHAT I NEED TO DO…NOW!"

We can hear God's Word from the mouth of God or we can hear God's Word from the mouth of the man of God or we can hear God's Word from our own mouth.

The words we speak out of our own mouths make a stronger, lasting impression on our Inside Man than the words other people speak to or about us. Granted, other people can say things to and about us that make a strong impact on our lives but the words of our own mouths resonate on our spirit and have a greater influence.

Yes, God has given us pastors to feed us with knowledge and understanding. How shall we hear without a preacher? However, as in the days of the Prophet Jeremiah, there are some pastors who have lost their minds. They no longer seek Godly wisdom and counsel and are ultimately, destroying God's vineyard (Jeremiah 10:21; 12:10).

> **"'What sorrow awaits the leaders of my people – the shepherds of my sheep – for they have destroyed and scattered the very ones they were expected to care for,' says the LORD."**
>
> **Jeremiah 23:1 NLT**

Satan has instituted a "catchall" strategy *in the church* to cast the net far and wide and "pull 'em in"…by any means necessary. Many men of God have been deceived to believe that "catching souls" – getting physical bodies to fill the church pews – is what's most important. But the Word of God says in Proverbs 11:30 (NIV)…

"He who wins souls is wise."

Souls were won in the early church because…*"They ceased not to teach and preach Jesus Christ"* (Acts 5:42)…

> **"How God anointed Jesus of Nazareth with the Holy Ghost and with power: who went about doing good, and healing all that were oppressed of the devil; for God was with him."**
>
> **Acts 10:38**

One of the major reasons we have not been able to effectively use our divine ammunition is because we have not consistently been given divine admonition.

Satan's biggest deliberate distraction in the body of Christ has been in the form of socially-acceptable messages that are being preached in lieu of spiritually-anointed messages; socially-acceptable messages that…

"..catch 'em but don't clean 'em".

As Disciples of Christ, we are fishers of men and our calling is to teach and preach spiritually-anointed messages that...

"...catch 'em AND clean 'em".

"Now ye are clean through the word which I have spoken unto you."
John 15:3

> *Socially-acceptable messages conform.*
> *Spiritually-anointed messages transform.*

Far too many men of God today are preaching socially-acceptable messages that *accommodate and enable* God's people when they should be preaching spiritually-anointed messages that *admonish and empower* God's people. With the prevalence of mega-churches, it is clear that the body of Christ is increasing in *quantity* but the preaching of these diluted, deceptive messages has been detrimental to the *quality* of the overall spiritual health and development of believers.

> *Socially-acceptable messages condone.*
> *Spiritually-anointed messages convict.*

The evidence is concrete. Week after week the pews of churches across the country, even across the world, are filled with fornicators, idolaters, adulterers, effeminate, abusers, thieves, envious, drunkards, hypocrites, and extortionists. On the one hand, that's exactly the way it's supposed to be. There is deliverance in the house of God.

Before we met, fell in love with and accepted Christ as our personal Savior and Lord, each one of us fell somewhere in between these commas (1 Corinthians 6:11).

Many of us are living proof that there is nothing too hard for the Lord; that there is no nut too hard for God to crack.

On the other hand, the gospel comes not simply with words, but also with power, with the Holy Spirit and with deep conviction (1 Thessalonians 1:5 NIV). The Spirit of Truth guides us into all truth…

> "…and *the truth shall make you free*…if the Son therefore shall make you free, ye shall be free indeed."
>
> John 8:32, 36

In today's society and in the church, these sins are being condoned because we have sought ungodly counsel and bought into the intellectual exposition of these behaviors as justification. We have allowed scholarly ethicality to supersede spiritual morality. Paul categorizes this behavior as unrighteous and forewarns us…

> "Know ye not that the unrighteous shall not inherit the kingdom of God? Be not deceived…"
>
> 1 Corinthians 6:9

Socially-acceptable messages compromise.
Spiritually-anointed messages challenge.

Compromise has taken up residence in the house of God. We've been deceived to believe that the end justifies the means; that a "little" compromise of who we are and what we stand for is okay because our endeavor is to reach out to a lost and dying world.

We've been deliberately distracted by the glitz and glitter of fame and have been deceived to believe that it's okay to bend and blend.

From my experience, if you bend something too much, eventually it will break. If you blend two different substances together, it taints the raw integrity of both substances. If you blend red paint with blue paint, you will no longer have pure red or blue paint, you will have purple paint. If you blend mix hot water with cold water, the water becomes lukewarm.

> *COMPROMISE will be our DEMISE.*

> **"But since you are like lukewarm water, neither hot nor cold, I will spit you out of my mouth!"**
>
> **Revelation 3:16 NIV**

If we don't get and stay divinely connected, we will do what seems right and appears straight but the end result will lead to death (Proverbs 16:25 AMP).

Remember, there still exists an individual responsibility because there exists an individual accountability (Romans 14:12).

Our primary reliance should be on the ministry of the Holy Spirit because He is the Teacher of the Truth, the whole Truth and nothing but the Truth.

> **"The Spirit shows what is true and will come and guide you into the full truth. The Spirit doesn't speak on his own. He will tell you only what he has heard from me, and he will let you know what is going to happen."**
>
> **John 16:13 CEV**

> *Socially-acceptable messages deceive.*
> *Spiritually-anointed messages deliver.*

I can't reiterate enough the importance of Step One: Master Your Mind. As we take personal time to study and meditate on God's Word, the Holy Spirit will minister to our spirit.

As the process of transformation commences and progresses, our spirit begins to agree with the Spirit of God and our thoughts begin to line up with God's thoughts and ultimately, our speech will line up with God's speech.

Now that's not to say that we should not hear what our preachers are saying because those who are called have been given a mandate to instruct God's people in the Word of God. BUT…and yes, there is a "but", we need to be very sure that *what* they are saying to us is what *God says* in His Word! We should only be following them *if* they are following Christ.

There are quite a few men of God in these days and times who are putting a twist on God's Word that is twisting the minds of God's people. Jesus says in Matthew 24:5 that many will come in His name and deceive many…

> **"Their impressive credentials and dazzling performances will pull the wool over the eyes of even those who ought to know better."**
>
> **Matthew 24:24 MSG**

Paul warns us…

> **"Let no man deceive you by any means…"**
>
> **2 Thessalonians 2:3**

The only way to circumvent deception is to secure our connection with the Power Source. When our relationship with the Holy Spirit is tight and right, He'll let us know what we need to know and when He does, we need to take heed.

Through his writings in the Psalm, King David demonstrates his understanding of the importance of mastering his mind to the Word of God. In Psalm 51:10 (CEV), he asks God to *"create pure thoughts in me, and make me faithful again."*

David recognized the inherent power of allowing God's Word to take root in his heart. If he was going to operate effectively and efficiently in his covenant with God, he knew that his heart had to be right with God.

David's "confession of faith" to Goliath during the infamous showdown in 1 Samuel 17:45-47 is proof positive that when God's Word takes root in our heart, we can speak to the giants in our life with boldness and confidence.

Do you consciously listen to your own daily conversation?

. . . .

Have you been boldly speaking life or death into your life?
Have you been speaking faith or are you speaking fear?
Are you dominating giants or are giants dominating you?

. . . .

If we are going to operate effectively and efficiently in our covenant with God, our heart has to be right with God so we can speak faith-filled, life-giving words that dominate the giants in our life.

The enemy is diligent and deliberate in his efforts to distract us from the Word of God. To ensure the optimal health of our spirit, we have to be diligent and deliberate in directing our focus to be firmly fixed on the Word of God; shifting our focus from our problems to God's promises. The Apostle Paul warns us not to…

> **"...look at the troubles we can see now; rather, we fix our gaze on things that cannot be seen. For the things we see now will soon be gone, but the things we cannot see will last forever."**
>
> 2 Corinthians 4:18 NLT

Everything we can see with our "natural" eye is temporary and subject to change by the things we can't see...our words. We may not be able to visibly "see" the words that come out of our mouth but when we speak the invisible everlasting Word of God over our life, there will be visible changes in our life.

God says in Jeremiah 23:28 (AMP)...

> **"...he who has My word, let him speak My word faithfully."**

God will not let one word we speak in faith fall to the ground. When we faithfully speak His Word over our life, He watches to see that His Word is fulfilled (Jeremiah 1:12). When we faithfully speak His Word over our life, we are forcing the undesirable things we see to line up until they become more desirable.

Because we are saying what He is saying about our life, we can *fully expect* His Word to change what we are seeing in our life; we *can fully expect* His Word to produce, to perform and to prosper in our lives.

When we realize how powerful our words really are, we might just consider going on a "tongue fast" until our mind has been renewed by the Word of God and our mouth has been refined by the Spirit of God.

DIVINE INTERVENTION

Not only does what we say have the power to change what we see in our lives, it has power to change what we see in the lives of others as well. The enemy doesn't stop at getting us to use our words to destroy just our own life; he gets us to use our words to destroy other people's lives as well...especially in the body of Christ.

> **"If you claim to be religious but *don't control your tongue*, you are fooling yourself, and your religion is worthless."**
>
> **James 1:26 NLT**

Let the people of God say...

"OUCH!!"

Tongue control, or more appropriately, lack of tongue control is a widespread dilemma in the body of Christ. This dilemma has resulted in the prevalent powerlessness that has made the body of Christ the laughing stock of the world.

This is one issue that should be but has not been acknowledged and addressed.

Lack of tongue control has caused pastors to deviate, churches to disband and members to disperse...disheartened. Lack of tongue control has driven both new believers away from God and detained "old" believers from returning to God. Lack of tongue control has created dysfunctional homes, disorderly families and dissolved marriages.

James provides an extensive exposé about the *nature* and *power* of the tongue in chapter 3...

> "A bit in the mouth of a horse controls the whole horse. A small rudder on a huge ship in the hands of a skilled captain sets a course in the face of the strongest winds. *A word out of your mouth may seem of no account, but it can accomplish nearly anything – or destroy it!*"
>
> James 3: 3-4 MSG

Just as the little bit – *a small metal mouthpiece of the bridle* – can control a large horse and a small rudder – *a vertically hinged plate that is mounted at the stern* – can set the course of a huge ship, our tiny tongue – *the muscle located between the small calcified whitish structures in our mouth* – can speak words that can control and set the course of an entire life.

Our tiny tongue has the ability to speak words that can enable us to *accomplish anything* or *destroy everything* in our life.

> "It only takes a spark, remember, to set off a forest fire. *A careless or wrongly placed word out of your mouth can do that.* By our speech we can ruin the world, turn harmony to chaos, throw mud on a reputation, send the whole world up in smoke and go up in smoke with it, *smoke right from the pit of hell.*"
>
> James 3:5-6 MSG

That's deep.

The parallel James makes between a *"careless or wrongly placed word"* that can change the entire course of one's life to a massive wildfire that has been kindled by a simple spark and destroyed thousands of acres of land, homes and in some cases, lives, is brilliant.

How many lives do you know that have been burnt because of something that's been said by an uncontrolled tongue?

If we were to align this parallel with our own life or the lives of people we know and love, we would realize, as I stated previously, that far too many lives have been altered in childhood and affected in adulthood by an angry word spoken to them by a loved one or a harsh word of chastisement uttered by a teacher or a slick word spoken in "jest" by a friend. All these words have made a tremendous impact and left a terrible imprint on their lives.

Oh, let's not forget words spoken by people with what they claim to be "innocent intent" – words that may seem of no account – but have caused more harm than good.

If I were a betting woman, I'd bet that more lives have been damaged by something someone said than by something someone did.

James goes on to say in verses 7 and 8…

> **"This is scary: You can tame a tiger, but *you can't tame a tongue*—it's never been done. The tongue runs wild, a wanton killer."**

The *King James Version* of James 3:8 – "*…but the tongue can no man tame; it is an unruly evil, full of deadly poison*" – corroborates the direct declaration in Proverbs 18:21 that "death" is in the power of our tongue.

If you've ever been privy to a shady conversation between a husband and wife or a parent and their child or an employer and their employee or one believer and another, or if you've ever been on the receiving end of such a conversation, then you know just how reckless and rude and how violent and venomous our tongues really are.

It's sad to say but there are more uncontrolled, uncontrollable tongues in the body of Christ than there should be.

For some reason, unbeknownst to me, Christians aka "followers of Christ" aka "believers" aka "church folk" tend to think that it's a-okay to say whatever they want to say, whenever they want to say it, however they want to say it to whomever they want to say it to. I'll tell you what…you haven't truly been ripped until you've been ripped by a "child of God".

Let the people of God say…

"OUCH!!"

The Master Design: Step Two

Our tongues were created to be a *creative force*. Yet more believers choose to use their tongue as a weapon of mass destruction. On any given day, they issue fierce tongue-lashings on others without any regard or regret about the consequence of their choice of words in their life or the lives of others. Strangely, these very same believers wonder why the blessings of the Lord are not flowing freely in their life.

People of God be not deceived, God is not mocked. As long as Earth lasts, you *will* reap what you sow.

If you continually sow hate and harm into someone else's life, you will reap a harvest of hate and harm into your own life. If you continually sow love and peace into someone else's life, you will reap a harvest of love and peace into your own life.

What goes around…comes around!

If we want more love, peace, joy, goodness and happiness to come around, we need to spread more love, peace, joy, goodness and happiness around.

> **"You are the salt of the earth. But what good is salt if it has lost its flavor?"**
> **Matthew 5:13 NLT**

When you place a tea bag into a cup of hot water and allow it to steep, the flavor in the bag is the flavor that seeps out of the bag. If you place a tea bag flavored with peppermint leaves into a cup of hot water, you will have a refreshing cup of peppermint tea. If you place a tea bag flavored with chamomile flowers, you will have a soothing cup of chamomile tea.

Exactly what happens when you place a tea bag into a cup of hot water is exactly what happens when believers are steeping in a "hot" situation.

Oh, we may be able to hide behind the mask with our eloquent, politically correct speech…temporarily but eventually, whatever flavor is in our heart is the flavor that will seep out of our mouth. If our heart is tart, our speech will breach the Word; if our heart is smart, our speech will be sweet and graciously seasoned with salt (Colossians 4:6 NIV).

I have personally witnessed church folk in a service where the Spirit was high, a rich word had been preached and a good song sung, running around the church, falling out, speaking in tongues and *"giving God all the glory, honor and praise due His name"*. But because their heart was tart, no sooner than service was over, these very same folk were the main ones gossiping about everything that happened in the service and everybody that happened to be doing anything in the service – right in church.

I know it to be true…because it's something I used to do.

I recall an incident at a church I had just started attending, where one of the members cautioned me to *"Be careful of these rattlesnakes."* Well, it wasn't long before I found out that she was the leader of the "rat pack".

Sadly, this type of conversation has become the norm in churches across the country – mini and mega. If this is the nature of the conversation that transpires between believers right in the House of God, one can only imagine the nature of their conversations in much less sacred settings.

Have you wondered why some members never seem to invite their family, friends or co-workers to church? My humble, educated guess would be that their family, friends and co-workers have no idea they even go to church. They might not even have a clue that they're Christians.

Let me ask you this: As an ambassador – a highly-esteemed, authorized representative of Christ sent by the government of God to represent the Kingdom of God during our temporary mission here on earth – would anyone standing within earshot of *your* conversations second-guess whose kingdom *you* were representing?

The Master Design: Step Two 155

James continues in verses 9 and 10 (MSG)...

> "**With our tongues we bless God our Father; with the same tongues we curse the very men and women he made in his image.** *Curses and blessings out of the same mouth!*"

MY...MY...MY!

Could this be where the cliché *"talking out of both sides of your mouth"* originated? Raise your hand if at some point in your Christian walk, you've been guilty of praising God out of one side of your mouth and cursing Brother BoBo and Sister So-and-So out of the other side of your mouth.

How can we, with a straight face, praise the Creator and curse His creation? How can we say we love the Creator with our praise yet curse His creation with our profanity!

The Word calls us LIARS!

> "**If anyone says, "I love God," yet hates his brother,** *he is a liar.* **For anyone who does not love his brother, whom he has seen, cannot love God, whom he has not seen."**
>
> **1 John 4:20 NIV**

* P A U S E   &   P O N D E R *

You might be thinking, *"Well, I wouldn't go so far to say that I hate my brothers and sisters in Christ."* YOU may not go so far as to say it but that's exactly what the Word went so far as to say.

"Love builds up" (1 Corinthians 8:1 NIV). If my memory serves me correctly, gossip has a reputation for tearing down. The opposite of building up is tearing down; the opposite of love (building up) is hate (tearing down).

Let the people of God say…

"OUCH!!"

Gossip is a deadly disease that has destroyed countless lives. Gossipers, who generally play judge and jury, either found these individuals guilty as charged, guilty by association, presumed innocent until proven guilty and then there were innocent bystanders who were pulled into the equation.

I once heard that gossip is hearing something negative that you like about someone you don't like. But it's goes much deeper than that. Gossip is hearing *anything* about *anybody* and spreading *everything* you heard to an irrelevant (or relevant) third party who, in turn, spreads it to another irrelevant (or relevant) party….and the beat goes on.

The official definition of gossip found on Dictionary.com is *"idle talk or rumor especially about the personal or private affairs of others"*.

"You must give an account on judgment day for every idle word you speak."

People gossip for various reasons but I believe that the most common reason people gossip is to deflect attention away from their messy lives. Their thinking is *"If people are talking about them, they won't be talking about me"*. Guess what, who gossips with you will gossip about you.

Billy Graham once said, *"A real Christian is the one who can give their pet parrot to the town gossip."*

The bottom line is this: blessings and curses should not be flowing so freely out of the same mouth of people who profess to follow Christ. If we are going to walk in the Light, we can't stay in darkness.

The great philosopher, Socrates had a noteworthy filter for gossip called *"Socrates Test of Three"*.

The first test was "truth". Are you absolutely certain that what you are about to tell me about this individual is true? The second test is "goodness". Are you about to tell me something good about this individual? The third test is the filter of "usefulness". Is what you want to tell me about this individual going to be useful to me?

My theory is this: if it sounds too good to be true, it probably is. Somewhere along the line somebody added some sugar and spice to make it sound nice. But even if it *is* true, if it's not good, what value does hearing something negative about someone else add to MY life? If what you're telling me about somebody else's "stuff" isn't going to change anything in my life, your life or their life, for that matter, for the better, why do I *need* to hear it?

Now that's not to say that sometimes I might not *want* to hear it (just because I'm being nosy – like most people) but I don't necessarily *need* to hear it.

Time spent listening to gossip is a waste of valuable time that could be used doing something useful. When we spend time listening to gossip, we are allowing someone to use us as human a "garbage dump" – depositing trash into our Inside Man. It's only a matter of time before we regurgitate the trash they deposited into our spirit into another willing receptacle. That's how the vicious cycle of gossip is perpetuated.

Come to think of it, the times I've "indulged" in the illicit, lewd act of gossip, nine times out of ten, the conversation was prefaced with *"Please don't repeat this to anybody."* The funny thing is the person who told that person probably said the exact same thing. It's the modern day equivalent of the age old question, *"Can you keep a secret?"*

In the words of Benjamin Franklin, *"three may keep a secret if two of them are dead."*

The natural wisdom of *Socrates Test of Three* is a twist on the Apostle Paul's spiritual wisdom found in Colossians 4:6 (MSG).

> **"Be gracious in your speech.** *The goal is to bring out the best in other*s **in a conversation, not put them down, not cut them out."**

People of God, the words that escape the oral cavity located on our facial region directly beneath the organ that facilitates smelling should *commend…not condemn*; they should *be tactful…not tacky*; they should be *gracious…not malicious*; they should *build up…not cut up*; they should *empower…not devour*.

> **"If you keep on biting and devouring each other, watch out or you will be destroyed by each other."**
>
> **Galatians 5:15 NIV**

You do realize that it's no coincidence that there are so many uncontrolled, uncontrollable tongues in the church, don't you? The enemy is a master strategist. He works smart…not hard.

He's had such great success using believers to sow discord among each other right in the church with the words of their mouth that he doesn't really even need to plant his demonic "moles" (but he does anyway). Because the issue of uncontrolled, uncontrollable tongues has not really been acknowledged and addressed, not only have we become accustomed to doing what we've been doing, we don't have a desire or even see the need to do something different or better.

Sowing discord is advantageous to the enemy; sowing discord is an abomination to God.

> **"There are six things the LORD hates – no, seven things he detests: haughty eyes, a lying tongue, hands that kill the innocent, a heart that plots evil, feet that race to do wrong, a false witness who pours out lies,** *a person who sows discord in a family.*
> **"**
>
> **Proverbs 6:16-19 NLT**

Isn't it interesting that four of the seven things mentioned in this passage of scripture that the Lord hates and considers despicable to Him are in some way connected to our mouth?

1. *A lying tongue…*

   "A lying tongue *hates* those it wounds and crushes."
   Proverbs 26:28 AMP

2. *A heart that plots evil…*

   "For from within, *out of a person's heart, come evil thoughts*, sexual immorality, theft, murder, adultery, greed, wickedness, deceit, lustful desires, envy, slander, pride, and foolishness. All these vile things come from within; they are what defile you."
   Mark 7:21-23 NLT

3. *A false witness…*

   "A false witness will not go unpunished, and he who pours out lies will perish."
   Proverbs 19:9 NIV

4. *One who sows discord…*

   "…wherever there is jealousy (envy) and contention (rivalry and selfish ambition), there will also be confusion (unrest, disharmony, rebellion) and all sorts of evil and vile practices."
   James 3:16 AMP

Our choice of words holds enormous significance in the eyes of God…and in the eyes of Satan. Both God and Satan know the power of the mind-mouth connection – that our thoughts become words and our words feed our thoughts.

Satan knows that as long as believers continue to sow *his* words in their life, there will be a harvest of deformation, not transformation. As long as believers continue to sow Satan's words in the lives of others, there will be a harvest of division, not unification. And guess what people of God…divided, we fall!

> "…every city or house divided against itself shall not stand."
>
> Matthew 12:25

Similarly, it is NOT okay to use foul language in or out of the pulpit. I know of a few good men and women of God who frequently use "curse words" to spice things up in their socially-acceptable messages. They even curse in casual conversation with their members!

Why would a man or woman of God who is called to bless God's people with the Word of God think it's acceptable or respectable to *curse* at the people of God? The shepherd of the house sets the protocol for the sheep in his pasture.

Of course, people who sit under this leadership have no problem with this type of behavior because the Word is being skewed to fit right snug with their lifestyle. This type of "teaching" gives them free rein to go right on "cussing" each other out, damning people and having God damn them as well.

It's no wonder the people of God are living in crisis!

*Cuss words are idle words…
and payday is on the way.*

Shepherds of the sheep, the words that come out of your mouth should encourage those who hear them to live a life that is pleasing to God, not encourage them to continue doing what they've already been doing.

> **"Let no foul or polluting language, nor evil word nor unwholesome or worthless talk [*ever*] come out of your mouth,** *but only such [speech] as is good and beneficial to the spiritual progress of others,* **as is fitting to the need and the occasion,** *that it may be a blessing and give grace (God's favor) to those who hear it.*
> **Ephesians 4:29 AMP**

The *Message Bible* sums it up to say...

> **"Watch the way you talk. Let nothing foul or dirty come out of your mouth.** *Say only what helps, each word a gift."*

Your words should convict them to modify their behavior so that it lines up with the Word of God, not convince them that their out of line behavior is acceptable.

God appointed you to shepherd His flock.

> **"His intention was the perfecting and the full equipping of the saints (His consecrated people), [that they should do] the work of ministering** *toward building up Christ's body (the church)*, **[That it might develop] until we all** *attain oneness in the faith..."*
> **Ephesians 4:11 AMP**

The job of a shepherd is to tend to, guide and protect His flock not give in to, divide and wreck His flock.

God is not pleased when those He appointed as shepherds of His flock abuse their position and misuse their power. He is not pleased when they are not faithful to fulfill their assignment in His divine order.

> "Therefore thus says the Lord, the God of Israel, concerning the shepherds who care for and feed My people: You have scattered My flock and driven them away and have not visited and attended to them; *behold, I will visit and attend to you for the evil of your doings*, says the Lord."
>
> **Jeremiah 23:2 AMP**

Jesus, the Good Shepherd, *"came down from heaven, not to do mine own will, but the will of him that sent me"* (John 6:38). God has appointed and anointed "under-shepherds" – men and women of God – not to do their own will but the will of Him that sent them.

"What Did Jesus Do"?

> "...for the works that the Father has appointed Me to accomplish and finish, the very same works that *I am now doing*."
>
> **John 5:36 AMP**

"What Did Jesus Say"?

> "For I did not speak of my own accord, but the Father who sent me *commanded me what to say and how to say it.*"
>
> **John 12:49 NIV**

The body of Christ is experiencing an unprecedented case of identity crisis and identity theft because some of these shepherds are not doing what Jesus did or saying what Jesus said.

But the responsibility doesn't rest on the shoulders of the shepherds alone. The sheep must make sure they are following a shepherd that is following the Good Shepherd. If they are not, it is the responsibility of the sheep to...

> "...intercede on their behalf, and give thanks for them. Pray this way for kings and all who are in authority so that we can live peaceful and quiet lives marked by godliness and dignity. This is good and pleases God our Savior, who wants everyone to be saved and to understand the truth."
>
> 2 Timothy 2:1-4 NLT

If the shepherd is following the Good Shepherd, it is the responsibility of the sheep to...

> "Obey your spiritual leaders, and do what they say. Their work is to watch over your souls, and they are accountable to God. Give them reason to do this with joy and not with sorrow. That would certainly not be for your benefit."
>
> Hebrews 13:17 NLT

It is also the responsibility of the sheep to not get caught up in the gulley of gossip. If we do what Jesus did and say what Jesus said like we are supposed to, we won't even have time to be in somebody else's business because we'll be about our Father's business – Kingdom business.

The best way to be in somebody else's business is to pray for them and ask God to show us how we can be of service...

> "The earnest prayer of a righteous person has great power and produces wonderful results."
>
> James 5:16 NLT

So NO, it is NOT okay to say whatever we want to say, whenever we want to say it, however we want to say it to whomever we want to say it to. It is NOT okay to curse at or cuss each other out – from the pulpit or anywhere else...in Jesus' name.

Now I'm sure I've stepped on a toe or two but it's the truth anyhow. Don't shoot the messenger. I'm just delivering the Spirit-inspired truth of God's message.

Think about this: What if God were to "go to the videotape" and playback our conversations on a Heavenly flat-screen? If we knew our conversation would be played back in surround sound for the entire world to hear, would we be more mindful about the content of our conversation?

> **"For all that is secret will eventually be brought into the open, and everything that is concealed will be brought to light and made known to all."**
>
> Luke 8:17 NLT

Let the people of God say...

"Uh-Oh!"

Next, James asks the question in verse 11 (NLT)...

> **"Does a spring of water bubble out with both fresh water and bitter water?"**

When we run hot water from a faucet, the longer it runs, the hotter it gets. The same goes for cold water; the longer it runs, the colder it gets. We cannot run hot and cold water simultaneously from the same faucet and preserve the stability of their temperature. The water will not be scalding hot nor will it be ice cold but lukewarm (and we know how Jesus feels about being lukewarm – Revelation 3:16).

Likewise, profanity and praise cannot flow simultaneously from the issues of our heart and preserve the stability of their influence. How much influence can your praise have on another believer who has heard you use profanity?

Praise that shares the same mouth with profanity is not a pure and powerful praise; it is a pretentious and polluted praise and God does not honor this type of praise offering.

Not only that, it confuses our spirit when praise and profanity flow simultaneously from our mouth.

"Surely, my brothers and sisters, this is not right!"

James 3:10 NLT

Remember, our spirit is not an interpreter, it is a facilitator. It's not going to try and figure out what we mean, it's going to try to make what we've said come to pass in our life.

When we go back and forth between blessing God and cursing man, our spirit becomes defiled and dysfunctional.

Technically, when we curse man, we curse God.

Why is any of this important? It's important because the Creator created us for His pleasure (Revelation 4:11). God is not pleased to hear us curse His creation. God is not pleased when we choose not to speak His Words of life over our life and the lives of others. Essentially, what we're telling Him is that we don't believe what He's said or that what He's said doesn't matter to us.

God *is* pleased when we PRESS in and PRAISE Him.

A PRESS in our spirit is an *active applied* faith – faith that knows *God already has*.

Praise is showing what our faith is knowing!

Imagine what would happen in the life of a believer who made a quality decision to consciously replace the "spirit of gossip" with a "spirit of praise" for the next thirty days.

MY...MY...MY!

You might be saying, *"I don't know if I can do that".*

You're right. You can't…not on your own. NO MAN can tame the tongue. James says it's humanly impossible.

A mastered mind thinks *"with God, ALL things are possible"*; a mastered mouth says, *"I can do all things through the anointing of the Anointed One."*

Our tongues can only be tamed by Divine intervention. Until we get connected and stay connected to the Power Source, the power in our "native" tongue will always produce sin and death and sickness and disease in our life.

No matter how hard we try to impress others with our elaborately-tailored speech, when the fire gets hot, our words will reveal the true character of who we really are behind the mask.

> *If our thinkin' is stinkin',*
> *our mouth will talk trash!*

If our heart is full of pollution, our mouth will speak profanity. If our heart is full of power, our mouth will speak praise. Proverbs 27:19 (NIV) says…

> **"As water reflects a face, so a man's heart reflects the man."**

To quote Elizabeth Kubler Ross…

> *People are like stained-glass windows.*
> *They sparkle and shine when the sun is out*
> *but when the darkness sets in, their true beauty*
> *is revealed only if there is light from within".*

When we receive the gift of salvation, God gives us a fresh start with a new heart. After our initial heart transplant, we must schedule frequent visits with the Master Cardiologist to preserve the purity of our hearts so we can tame the tartness in our tongues.

King David was a man after God's own heart (Acts 13:22). As we read through the book of Psalms, the primary theme is clear – David was very concerned with the condition of his heart and stayed connected to God to ensure that his heart was conditioned to function properly.

> **"Let the words of my mouth, and the meditation of my heart, be acceptable in thy sight, O LORD, my strength, and my redeemer."**
> **Psalm 19:14**

> **"Put me on trial, Lord, and cross-examine me. Test my motives and my heart."**
> **Psalm 26:2 NLT**

> **"Create in me a clean heart, O God; and renew a right spirit within me."**
> **Psalm 51:10**

> **"If I had not confessed the sin in my heart, the Lord would not have listened."**
> **Psalm 66:18 NLT**

David's praise was *profuse* because his heart was *primed*.

> **"The Lord is my Strength and my [impenetrable] Shield; my heart trusts in, relies on, and confidently leans on Him, and I am helped; therefore my heart greatly rejoices, and with my song will I praise Him."**
> **Psalm 28:7 AMP**

David's praise was *profound* because his heart was *sound*.

> **"My heart is confident in you, O God; my heart is confident. No wonder I can sing your praises."**
> **Psalm 57:7 NLT**

David's praise was an outward expression of the indwelling of God's abundant love in his heart.

It is clear that King David imparted and instilled the importance of having a pure heart condition to his son, as we find Solomon admonishing us in Proverbs 4:23 (NLT) to...

> **"Guard your heart above all else, for it determines the course of your life."**

There is a strong heart-mind-mouth connection in the book of Proverbs. Immediately following his admonition in verse 23, Solomon cautions us in verse 24...

> **"Avoid all perverse talk; stay away from corrupt speech."**

He goes on to say in Proverbs 16:23 (NIV)...

> **"A wise man's heart guides his mouth, and his lips promote instruction."**

I particularly like the *New Living Translation's* rendition...

> **"From a wise mind comes wise speech; the words of the wise are persuasive."**

King Solomon, the second wisest man that ever lived, has much to say and gives sound counsel concerning the "fruit of our lips".

Reading through the numerous scriptures that relate to the heart-mind-mouth connection in Proverbs alone should give us a clear indication that our words have a direct impact on our life.

> **"Those who control their tongue will have a long life; opening your mouth can ruin everything."**
>
> **Proverbs 13:3 NLT**

> "Watch your words and hold your tongue, you'll save yourself a lot of grief."
>
> **Proverbs 21:23 MSG**

Solomon's advice in Proverbs 6:2 (AMP)...

> "You are snared with the words of your lips, you are caught by the speech of your mouth."

...confirms Jesus' counsel in Matthew 12:37 (AMP)...

> "For by your words you will be justified and acquitted, and by your words you will be condemned and sentenced."

Don't you find it interesting that Jesus says *our words* – not our thoughts, not our actions – but *our words* will free or frame us, deliver or damn us, pardon or punish us.

Let the people of God say...

"HMM!!"

Proverbs 10:11 tells us that *"The words of the godly are a life-giving fountain."* Jesus echoes this proverb in John 6:63 (MSG)...

> "Every word I've spoken to you is a Spirit-word, and so it is life-making."

If you recall those credible catchphrases and chichi clichés that the enemy has successfully programmed into our speech, you will recognize that they are all words that produce death – not life.

For the longest time, people have been wondering why God allowed this or that to happen in their life.

Let the people of God say...

GOD ALLOWS WHAT WE ALLOW.

It may sound ludicrous…but it is what it is.

God *has given us* the authority over ALL the power of enemy and that authority is activated when we choose to speak His words of life. When we exercise our right and speak God's Word in faith over our life, we are agreeing with what He's already said about us. When we agree with God, it allows or enables Him to perform His Word on our behalf.

When we speak faith-filled words over our life even in the midst of catastrophic circumstances, we allow God the freedom to accomplish what He pleases in our life…His divine design of an abundant life of power, peace and prosperity.

However, when we pass our baton of dominion to Satan by speaking fear-filled words that we know are not of God, we disallow or disable God from taking any action on our behalf. He is under no obligation to intervene on our behalf when we speak words of death because those words are not His words. He says in Jeremiah 1:12 that He watches over *His Word* to see that it is fulfilled.

Therefore, He *must allow* the fear-filled words that we speak to come to pass in our life because 1) He is obligated to His Word and 2) He delegated that authority to us.

Let us not forget to remember the choice we've been given in Deuteronomy 30:19 (NLT).

> **"Today *I have given you the choice* between life and death, between blessings and curses. Now I call on heaven and earth to witness the choice you make. *Oh, that you would choose life*, so that you and your descendants might live!"**

Let us not forget to remember the delegation of power we received in Luke 10:19 (AMP).

> **"Behold! *I have given you authority and power* to trample upon serpents and scorpions, and [physical and mental strength and ability] over all the power that the enemy [possesses]; and nothing shall in any way harm you."**

Let us not forget to remember that the choice we've been given and the delegation of power we've received is activated or deactivated by our choice of words.

> **"Death and life are in the power of the tongue, and they who indulge in it shall eat the fruit of it [for death or life]."**
> Proverbs 18:21 AMP

When we gain a better appreciation for the power of our words, we will understand the "weightiness" of speaking idle words.

Life and death are in the power of our tongue. Blessing and curses are in the power of our tongue. Every word we speak produces either life and blessings or death and curses in our life.

Hosea 4:6 tells us that the people of God are destroyed because we lack knowledge. We are destroyed because we are ignorant when it comes to the things of God as they pertain to life and godliness.

Our lack of knowledge is not due to the lack of availability of knowledge because knowledge is readily available to us in God's Word. Rather, our lack of knowledge stems from our lack of individual responsibility to acquire that knowledge.

Although numerous books – both spiritual and secular – have been penned on the topic of the power of our words, the people of God remain ignorant and inactive.

Solomon says…

> **"The mouths of fools are their ruin; they trap themselves with their lips."**
> Proverbs 18:7 NLT

Some believers foolishly say what they want to say because they lack knowledge concerning the colossal power in our words. They carelessly bless God and curse fellow believers because they lack knowledge concerning the law of sowing and reaping.

Others have this knowledge yet refuse to put it to work in their life. Knowing what to do and not doing it is worse than not knowing at all. Knowing what to do and not doing it is blatant disobedience.

Blatant mistrust and disobedience is the number one reason believers who are not receiving the promises of God are not receiving the promises of God.

If you are really ready to walk in God's divine design for our life on this earth, schedule an emergency appointment with the Master Cardiologist for radical open heart surgery.

Your pre-surgical plea should be...

> **"Search me, O God, and know my heart; test me and know my anxious thoughts. *Point out anything in me that offends you*, and lead me along the path of everlasting life."**
>
> **Psalm 139:23, 24 NLT**

As we allow the Master Cardiologist to purge and purify our hearts and allow the Chief Speech Pathologist to eradicate and elucidate our speech disorder, we will come into that spirit of unity in the faith and in the knowledge of His Son that God desires. Only then will we become fully developed disciplined disciples so that with *one heart and mouth* we can be about our Father's business – sharing the love of Jesus with a dying world and winning the lost at any cost.

People of God, Divine intervention is what it's going to take to correct our disturbing dialect so we can effectively use our divine ammunition against the forces of evil in our life and see the promises of God come to fruition in our life.

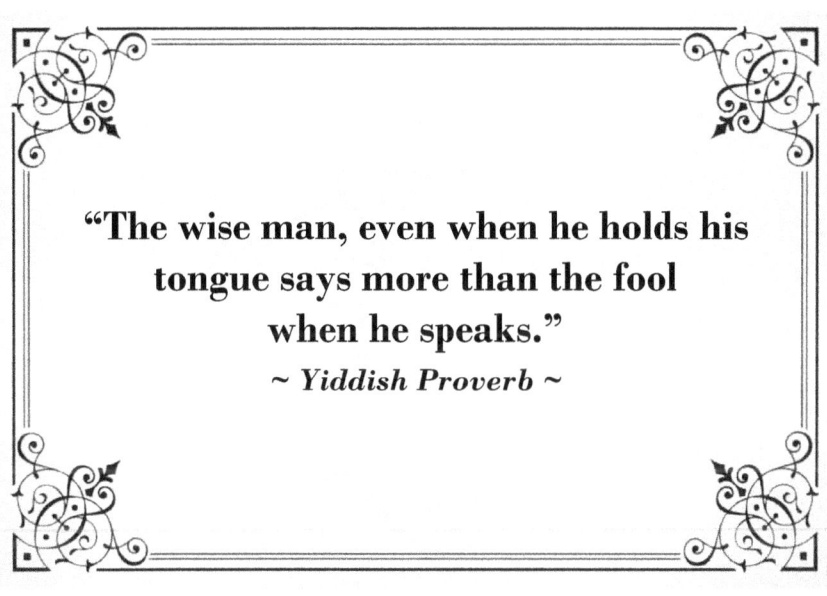

"The wise man, even when he holds his tongue says more than the fool when he speaks."
~ *Yiddish Proverb* ~

Step Three:
Master Your Money

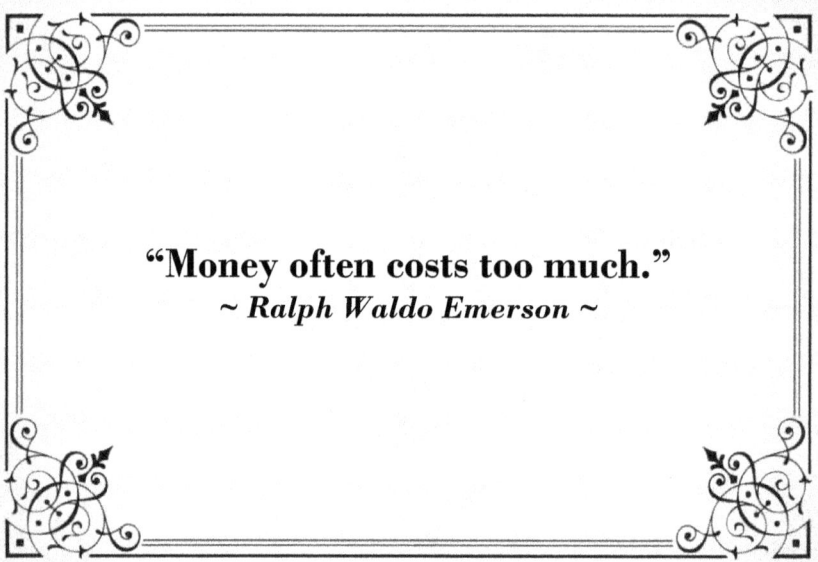

"Money often costs too much."
~ *Ralph Waldo Emerson* ~

DECEPTIVE DATA DISPELLED

      Long before this economic earthquake shook the financial foundation of the free world, there were lots of believers who were financially challenged and living in crisis. This financial deficiency had nothing to do with this world's economy because believers are not restricted to operating under this earthly economy; we have been granted unlimited access to the heavenly economy.

      No, this financial deficiency had everything to do with a spiritual deficiency that originated in part from the dissemination of deceptive data.

      For quite some time, believers have been receiving deceptive data that has led us to believe that financial prosperity is NOT the will of God for His people. This deceptive data is deeply rooted in an old religious myth that money is the root of all evil.

      It is very unfortunate that many believers have accepted this myth as a matter of fact and have been living life as paupers, in crisis, when our true calling is to live life as princes, *in Christ*.

1 Timothy 6:10 is possibly one of *the* most misquoted scriptures in the Word of God. It is frequently misquoted by religious people who don't have much money, possibly to justify their lack of it or by religious leaders who have indoctrinated religious people to believe that poverty is a sign of humility and humility is a sign of holiness.

Sadly, the "mis-indoctrination" of 1 Timothy 6:10 has kept more folk broke – pinching pennies and trying to make a dollar out of fifteen cents – than a little bit.

Unlike Proverbs 18:21 and Romans 10:17, most believers believe that 1 Timothy 6:10 begins where *their* recitation begins.

It does not.

Money, in and of itself, is NOT the root of all evil.

Isn't it amazing how eliminating any portion in a passage of scripture puts a totally different spin on it?

To the naked eye, the prime focus of this scripture is that money is the root of all evil. To the newborn eye whose vision has been corrected by the Spirit of God and who reads the passage of scripture in context, the prime focus of this scripture is about messed up mindsets motivated by money.

If we back up a few verses and read this passage in context, we find the Apostle Paul in verses 3-5 admonishing his spiritual son, Timothy, to teach what he's been taught – the unadulterated, uncompromised Word of God. Paul is cautioning Timothy to beware of so-called men of God who, because of their arrogance and ignorance, teach messages that contradict the Word and cause controversy and chaos.

They're not interested in teaching the people of God sound instruction that promotes godly living.

Their primary interest is using their prestigious position as a source for financial gain.

I personally know one man who publicly declared, *"If you want to be rich, become a pastor"*.

And that he did.

Paul goes on to say in verses 6-9 (CEV):

> **"And religion does make your life rich, by making you content with what you have. We didn't bring anything into this world, and we won't take anything with us when we leave. So we should be satisfied just to have food and clothes. People who want to be rich fall into all sorts of temptations and traps. They are caught by foolish and harmful desires that drag them down and destroy them."**

Paul's exposé in 1 Timothy 6:6-9 alludes to Jesus' exposition in Matthew 6:19-24 (MSG).

> **"Don't hoard treasure down here where it gets eaten by moths and corroded by rust or—worse!—stolen by burglars. Stockpile treasure in heaven, where it's safe from moth and rust and burglars. It's obvious, isn't it?** *The place where your treasure is, is the place you will most want to be, and end up being.*"

Jesus concludes His exposition in Matthew 6:33 by encouraging us to passionately pursue an intimate One-on-one relationship with God...*above all else.*

RELATIONSHIP IS THE KEY
Religion without relationship makes like rigid.
Religion with relationship makes like rich.

When we are engaged in an intimate One-on-one relationship with God – not the customary one out of seven day deal, it changes our perspective about everything, including money.

What 1 Timothy 6:10 does say is that *the love of* money is the root of all evil.

- The *love of* money is responsible for the misinformation being exchanged through multimedia & misinterpretations being entertained by the masses.

- The *love of* money is responsible for the misappropriation and mismanagement of funds in the financial forum.

- The *love of* money is responsible for the miscalculations in business deals and misunderstandings in professional relationships.

- The *love of* money is responsible for the misapplication of finances and mistrust running rampant in the body of Christ.

- *The love of* money is responsible for the misconduct in far too many marriages and the resulting misfortune of broken homes.

- *The love of* money is responsible for the misdirection and misbehavior of our children.

The love of money – our mindset regarding money – is the real issue at hand in 1 Timothy 6:10.

In the past decade or so, there has been a widespread outbreak of socially-acceptable messages being preached in the body of Christ. "Men of God" with money-motivated mindsets, who have chosen to worship the almighty dollar rather than worship Almighty God, are preaching socially-acceptable messages that dilute and pollute God's truth concerning divine prosperity.

Audaciously, they paint a tainted picture of God's Master plan which explores and implores the unscriptural notion of "buying a breakthrough". You know, *"throw a dollar and holla"* and God will give you everything you want. These socially-acceptable messages are keeping the people of God bound in the pothole of poverty.

> **"You hypocrites! Isaiah was right when he prophesied about you, for he wrote, 'These people honor me with their lips, but their hearts are far from me. Their worship is a farce, for *they teach man-made ideas as commands from God*.'"**
>
> **Mark 7:6-7 NLT**

The main reason so many are opposed to the prosperity message as it is being preached in socially-acceptable messages is because it isolates and elevates financial prosperity. Its premise is that living an abundant life is *"all about the Benjamins"*.

It is not.

Financial prosperity is a by-product of divine prosperity; it is secondary not primary. True financial prosperity can never be obtained without first attaining spiritual maturity. Spiritual maturity is the infrastructure for genuine prosperous living.

Let the people of God say...

"THAT'S GOD DIVINE ORDER."

Spiritually-anointed messages give sound instruction in the area of financial prosperity teaching the people of God why it is imperative that we assume fiscal responsibility of all God has entrusted us with *and* how to do so in a way that honors and glorifies God.

Authentic abundant life transcends the financial frontier; it embraces every area of our life – spiritual, mental, emotional, physical, familial, professional, recreational and social...not just financial.

Finances are only one slice of the abundant life pie. Perhaps the financial slice is most dominant because it is the most "tangible" and touches every area of our life.

An authentic abundant life is a life of holiness and wholeness. A life of holiness – *one that is consecrated for and concentrated on the things of God* breeds a life of wholeness – *a life where nothing is missing and nothing is broken in any area of our life.*

That this misconception has sparked such dissension in the body of Christ should compel believers to diligently seek the wisdom of God concerning His take on the matter.

> **"My advice is wholesome. There is nothing devious or crooked in it. My words are plain to anyone with understanding, clear to those with knowledge."**
>
> **Proverbs 8:8-9 NLT**

Diligently seeking the wisdom of God does not apply solely to the prosperity message. Any topic that you may need clarity on due to misinterpretations and misconceptions should be subject to further investigation.

Spiritual negligence is prevailing in the body of Christ because believers have become accustomed to being "spoon-fed". Believers have become so enamored by the "messenger" that they accept their messages without question.

Satan's master plan for God's people is to create disorder through perversion. His words are corrupt and leave people confounded.

1 John 4:1 (NLT) tells us *"do not believe everyone who claims to speak by the Spirit. You must test them to see if the spirit they have comes from God."* The *Message Bible* bluntly says.

> **"Don't believe everything you hear. Carefully weigh and examine what people tell you. Not everyone who talks about God comes from God. There are a lot of lying preachers loose in the world."**

Paul urges us in Romans 16:17 and 18 (NIV) to...

"...watch out for those who cause divisions and put obstacles in your way that are contrary to the teaching you have learned. Keep away from them. For such people are not serving our Lord Christ, but their own appetites. *By smooth talk and flattery they deceive the minds of naive people.*"

In the early church, although the Bereans received Paul and Silas' message with great enthusiasm, they *"examined the Scriptures every day to see if what Paul said was true"* (Acts 17:11 NIV).

It all points back to God's instruction in Joshua 1:8 and Jesus' counsel in Matthew 6:33 to...

> *"Study this Book of Instruction continually."*
> *"Seek the Kingdom of God above all else."*

Before I continue, let me be clear that this is NOT a campaign to degrade, diminish or denounce God's anointed (I know better); this *is* a campaign to persuade, provoke and petition the people of God to take *personal responsibility* for their soul salvation because at the end of the day, we must ALL face the music (Romans 14:12).

God has anointed and appointed these men and women in this position of authority for our good and we are required to submit to their authority (Romans 13:1).

It's a good thing to establish a stable relationship with God's servants who instruct us about His will and His ways but it's an even better thing to establish an intimate One-on-one relationship with God.

Believers have become so reliant on the messenger, the servant of God, that they have little or no regard for the Messenger, the Spirit of God.

Believers attend particular churches based solely on their "relationship" with the Pastor when we really should be attending church solely based on our relationship with God.

A divine connection with the man of God is no substitution for a divine connection with the Spirit of God.

Susceptibility to deception and distraction increases when our divine connection is severed or short-circuited but when our divine connection is secure and sound, our vulnerability dissolves because the Spirit of truth will guide us into the whole truth and nothing but the truth (John 16:13).

God's Master Plan for His people is one of divine order and precision. His Word is clear and concise.

Our Father's Master Plan for His people is for us…

- *To have dominion…not be dominated.*

    "You made him to have dominion over the works of Your hands; You have put all things under his feet."

    Psalm 8:6 AMP

- *To live life by His divine design…not by default.*

    "I came that they may have and enjoy life, and have it in abundance (to the full, till it overflows)."

    John 10:10 AMP

- *To be prosperous…not pitiful.*

    "Beloved, I wish above all things that thou mayest prosper and be in health, even as they soul prospereth."

    3 John 2

Our Father's Master Plan of divine prosperity for His people encompasses a prosperous spirit, a prosperous soul and a prosperous body...not just a prosperous bank account. It doesn't exclude a prosperous bank account but it is not exclusively limited to a prosperous bank account.

Socially-acceptable messages have kindled immense excitement among the people of God about the *prospect* of living in the overflow.

"I bear them witness that they have a [certain] zeal and enthusiasm for God, but it is not enlightened and according to [correct and vital] knowledge."

Romans 10:2 AMP

Unfortunately, excitement alone will not create the experience. If it did, every excited believer would be experiencing overflow in their life right now.

And here's the thing: the devil is just as excited as we are about the *prospect* of living in the overflow. As long as we don't earnestly pursue the promise, he's as excited as a kid in a video game store. However, as our zeal and enthusiasm is enlightened according to correct and vital knowledge and we pursue the promise and begin to experience what we've been excited about, *his* excitement will dissipate.

This is a critical issue because right here is where many believers are missing it and missing out on the promise of living in "John 10:10 overflow"... in this life.

As believers, we *should be* excited about expecting to experience God's promises in this life. Proverbs 10:28 tells us the expectation of the righteous brings joy. But at some point, we need to transition from *"expecting to experiencing"*.

Let the people of God say...

"I AM EXPERIENCING GOD'S PROMISES IN MY LIFE...NOW!"

This transition from *expecting to experiencing* can only transpire through transformation.

Transformation only transpires when we consistently commune with God to gain an intimate knowledge about Who He really is and what He's already done for us *in Christ*. This communion will renew our minds and transform our thinking to the understanding that financial prosperity IS the will of God for His children.

If you seriously contemplate the validity of the premise that financial prosperity is NOT the will of God for His children, you would realize that it really doesn't make much sense at all.

This line of thinking – or more appropriately, out of line thinking – is totally contrary to God's divine design of an abundant life of power, peace and prosperity for His people.

Why would El Shaddai, the All-Sufficient God Who is *more than enough* want His children to settle with *not enough* or be satisfied with *just enough*?

> *How can we have dominion in our lives if lack is dominating our lives?*

We were created for God's pleasure (Revelation 4:11) and our Father takes pleasure in the prosperity of His children (Psalm 35:27).

Think about it: "John 10:10 overflow" is not on reserve until we get to Heaven; "John 10:10 overflow" is for here and now.

"John 10:10 overflow" IS God's divine design!

Let the people of God say…

"I'M LIVING IN 'JOHN 10:10 OVERFLOW'!"

The twenty-third Psalm is a familiar passage of scripture that is frequently quoted but may not be fully comprehended. As a descendant of Abraham, David's confession – *"The LORD is my shepherd; I shall not want"* – proves that he had a personal knowledge of God as Jehovah-Jireh. His declaration – *"My cup overflows with blessings"* – avows that he had a personal encounter with "the Lord Who provides."

Paul substantiates David's stance with yet another frequently quoted, clearly not fully comprehended passage of scripture…

"And my God *will liberally supply* (fill to the full) your every need according to His riches in glory in Christ Jesus."
Philippians 4:19 AMP

Both passages of scripture depict God as being a generous and giving Father to His children – NOT a miserly and mean Man. He is NOT trying to withhold any *good thing* from those who do the right thing (Psalm 84:11). His desire is to bestow *every good and perfect gift* upon us (James 1:17).

The Best, most Perfect Gift God ever gave us was wrapped in swaddling clothes lying in a manger. God gave us Jesus that we might secure our eternal destiny with Him *and* that we might enjoy a rich and satisfying earthly destiny in Him.

Suffice it to say, Jesus' proclamation in John 10:10 alone dispels the deceptive data being disseminated that financial prosperity is NOT the will of God for His people.

Now there are those who may refute my claim by asserting that these scriptures are not speaking specifically about financial prosperity but spiritual blessings. Well, let's delve a little deeper in the Word and see if we can "connect the dots".

In the opening of his letter to the church at Ephesus (1:3 NIV), after his preliminary salutation of *"Grace and Peace"* to the faithful followers of the Lord Jesus Christ, Paul continues with a praise offering to the God and Father of our Lord Jesus Christ…

> "…who has blessed us in the heavenly realms with every spiritual blessing *in Christ.*"

What are these spiritual blessings that we are now recipients of? Paul's provides insight in his dissertation in Ephesians 1:4-14 (NLT).

- **Selection:** "Even before he made the world, God loved us and *chose us* in Christ to be holy and without fault in his eyes." (v4)

- **Adoption:** "God decided in advance to *adopt us* into his own family by bringing us to himself through Jesus Christ." (v5)

- **Recognition:** "So we praise God for the glorious grace he has poured out on us *who belong* to his dear Son." (v6)

- **Redemption:** "He is so rich in kindness and grace that he *purchased our freedom* with the blood of his Son…" (v7)

- **Exoneration:** "…and *forgave our sins.*" (v7)

- **Compassion:** "He has showered his *kindness on us…*" (v8)

- **Comprehension:** "…along with all *wisdom and understanding.*" (v8)

- **Revelation:** "God has now *revealed to us* his mysterious plan regarding Christ, a plan to fulfill his own good pleasure." (v9)

- **Possession:** "…because we are united with Christ, we have *received an inheritance* from God, for he chose us in advance, and he makes everything work out according to his plan." (v11)

- **Authentication:** "*The Spirit is God's guarantee* that he will give us the inheritance he promised and that he has purchased us to be his own people." (v14)

Paul continues to chronicle our spiritual blessings *in Christ* in other letters…

- **Salvation:** "For God *chose to save us* through our Lord Jesus Christ…" (1 Thessalonians 5:9 NLT).

- **Justification:** "*[All] are justified* and made upright and in right standing with God, freely and gratuitously by His grace (His unmerited favor and mercy), through the redemption which is [provided] in Christ Jesus" (Romans 3:24 AMP).

- **Sanctification:** "…*we are sanctified* through the offering of the body of Jesus Christ once for all" (Hebrews 10:10).

- **Reconciliation:** "But all things are from God, Who through Jesus Christ *reconciled us to Himself* [received us into favor, brought us into harmony with Himself]…" (2 Corinthians 5:18 AMP).

- **New Creation:** "…anyone who belongs to Christ has become a new person. The old life is gone; a *new life has begun*" (2 Corinthians 5:17 NLT).

- **Elevation:** And *God raised us up with Christ* and seated us with him in the heavenly realms in Christ Jesus" (Ephesians 2:6 NIV).

Our unity with Christ affords us accessibility to *every* one of these spiritual blessings…and so many more.

By the same token, our unity with Christ affords us accessibility to financial blessings.

Paul writes in his letter to the church at Galatia…

> "**And *now that you belong to Christ*, you are the true children of Abraham. You are his heirs, and *God's promise to Abraham belongs to you*.**"
>
> Galatians 3:29 NLT

Now that we belong to Christ, the promises God made to Abraham belong to us! That means everything God promised Abraham has been passed down to us through Christ!

> "**The promises were spoken to Abraham and to his seed. The Scripture does not say "and to seeds," meaning many people, but "and to your seed," meaning one person, who is Christ.**"
>
> Galatians 3:16 NIV

Lately, there has been much ado about the "blessing of Abraham". Well exactly what did God promise Abram?

> "**Now the LORD had said unto Abram, Get thee out of thy country, and from thy kindred, and from thy father's house, unto a land that I will shew thee: And I will make of thee a great nation, and I will bless thee, and make thy name great; and thou shalt be a blessing: And I will bless them that bless thee, and curse him that curseth thee: and in thee shall all families of the earth be blessed.**"
>
> Genesis 12:1-3

Essentially, the blessing of Abraham consists of five distinctive promises:

1. TERRITORIAL PROMISE (GENESIS 12:1)

God commanded Abram to move out of his native soil, away from his relatives, away from his father's house *"to a land that I will show you"*. Without hesitation, Abram obeyed God's command taking his wife, Sarai, his nephew, Lot and everything they owned and headed to the land of Canaan.

Upon his arrival in Canaan in verse 7, the Lord appeared to Abram again to clarify and ratify this territorial promise.

"I will give this land to your descendants".

This territorial promise, which was fulfilled when the children of Israel possessed the land of Canaan under Joshua's leadership, is still in full effect today. In modern day America, Abraham's descendants own more real estate than any other ethnic group. There is a large Jewish presence in my old Brooklyn neighborhood. Every now and then I would see them walking continually around in certain areas…"possessing the land" in accordance with Deuteronomy 11:24 (AMP) which says *"Every place upon which the sole of your foot shall tread shall be yours."*

2. NATIONAL PROMISE (GENESIS 12:2)

God then promised to make Abram *"a great nation."* When Jacob journeyed to the land of Egypt with his family, Genesis 46:27 says they were seventy in number. When Moses addressed the children of Israel in Deuteronomy 1:10-11 (NLT)…

> **"The LORD your God has increased your population, *making you as numerous as the stars*! And may the LORD, the God of your ancestors, *multiply you a thousand times more and bless you as he promised*!"**

The territorial and national promises God made to Abram still stand strong as God continues to multiply and exceedingly bless his descendants.

3. Financial Promise (Genesis 12:2)

Abram was already *"very rich in cattle, in silver, and in gold"* (Genesis 13:2). In fact, Abram and Lot had so much that *"the land could not support them while they stayed together, for their possessions were so great"* (Genesis 13:6 AMP).

But here we find God promising to bless Abram *"with abundant increase of favors"*. We know that this abundant increase of favors included finances because Genesis 24:1 tells us that *"the LORD had blessed Abraham in all things"*.

God blessed Abram with more than enough so he could be a blessing *"dispensing good to others."*

4. Provisional Promise (Genesis 12:3)

The provision is simple: *"I will bless anyone who blesses you, but I will put a curse on anyone who puts a curse on you."* (CEV) Many people do not comprehend the importance in blessing Israel as well as the body of Christ (Galatians 3:29). It may appear that the severe wrath that Israel is experiencing at the hands of her enemies and the relentless ridicule being heaped on the body of Christ is prevailing but be very sure that it is not.

We need not fret because of evildoers. Instead we should…

> **"Wait for and expect the Lord and *keep and heed His way*, and He will exalt you to inherit the land; [in the end] when the wicked are cut off, you shall see it."**
>
> **Psalm 37:34 AMP**

5. Spiritual Promise (Genesis 12:3)

This word of promise was spoken to Abram and Christ. Galatians 3:16 (NIV) tells us that…*"The promises were spoken to Abraham and to his seed. The Scripture does not say "and to seeds," meaning many people, but "and to your seed," meaning one person, who is Christ."*

Indeed God blessed Abram and his descendents to experience the territorial, national, provisional and financial promises but this spiritual promise could only be fulfilled *in Christ* (Ephesians 1:3).

Galatians 3:29 says that now that we belong to Christ, we are children and heirs of Father Abraham and God's promise to Abraham belongs to us – *territorial, national, financial, provisional and spiritual.*

For those who have lost homes in the wake of this economic earthquake, I say to you walk in your *territorial blessing.* Just as Joshua led the children of Israel into the Promised Land, Jesus has led us to our Promised Land to live in houses we did not build, houses filled with all kinds of good things we did not provide, wells we did not dig, and vineyards and olive groves we did not plant (Deuteronomy 6:10-11 NIV).

For those who have lost families through divorce and dysfunction, I say to you walk in your *national blessing.* Our family is "our nation". The promise of restoration belongs to us. God promised to restore the years that the locust has eaten (Joel 2:25) and the glory of this latter house will be greater than the former (Haggai 2:9). All your children shall be taught of the Lord and great shall be their peace (Isaiah 54:13).

What shall we say for those who have been wrongfully accused and abused and misused, walk in your *provisional blessing…"Do not take revenge, my friends, but leave room for God's wrath, for it is written: 'It is mine to avenge; I will repay,' says the Lord"* (Romans 12:19 NIV).

For those who may be wondering *"What kind of God would forgive ME after all I've done?"* I say to you walk in your *spiritual blessing* of Salvation, Justification, Sanctification, Reconciliation, New Creation and Elevation! El Malei Rachamim is the All-Merciful God.

> **"It is because of His mercies that we are not consumed because *His compassions fail not. They are new every morning*: great is thy faithfulness."**
>
> **Lamentations 3:22-23**

For those of you who have been financially challenged for reasons known only to you and God, walk in your *financial blessing* and trust God to generously provide all you need. Not only will He increase your resources, He will also produce a great harvest of generosity in you (2 Corinthians 9:8-10 NLT).

People of God, God's divine design for us is that we live an abundant life of power, peace, and prosperity and He's already done what He needed to do to make sure that we have everything we need to walk in His divine design.

Let the people of God say…

"I AM LIVING GOD'S DIVINE DESIGN!"

Pardon my digression but I needed to dispel the deceptive data that's been disseminated that *financial prosperity* is NOT the will of God for His people. And just as in the early days of the church, some will believe the things that have been spoken and some will not (Acts 28:24).

It is NOT the will of God for His people to be broke. I've been broke before and I'm here to let you know, as corny as it may sound, being broke ain't no joke. If you've ever been broke then you know that I am telling the truth.

Being broke breeds a life of mediocrity that breeds a life of limited choices that breeds a life of crisis that breeds a life of stress.

We've already ascertained that being stressed is NOT the will of God which validates my point that being broke is NOT the will of God for His people.

Being broke breeds everything opposite of what God's divine design breeds. Being blessed breeds an awesome quality of life – a tranquil, stress-free life filled with infinite choices.

This is not to say that we will never experience tribulation in our life. Jesus said in John 16:33 (AMP)... *"In this world you will have tribulation and trials and distress and frustration..."* but in Him, we can have peace and take courage, be confident, certain and undaunted in the midst of it all because He has *already* overcome – triumphed over, conquered and defeated – the world!

Let the people of God say...

"I AM A WORLD OVERCOMER!"

Why is it so difficult for us to believe that God has blessed us immensely *in Christ*? What kind of Father wants to see His children broke and struggling? As a parent, does it bring you pleasure to see your child broke and struggling? Likewise, it does not bring God pleasure to see His children broke and struggling. He wants us to live an abundant life of power, peace and prosperity just like we want to see our children living successful, prosperous lives.

But in both scenarios, the struggle begins because of the choices we make. When our children choose to do things that land them in unpleasant predicaments, sometimes we can't help them. We have to just let the situation run its course. Likewise, when we choose to do things that land us in unpleasant predicaments, sometimes God can't help us. He has to just let the situation run its course.

Believers are not broke because it's God's will; believers are broke because they refuse to follow God's way.

God doesn't punish His people with poverty. It saddens me when I hear people blame God for things that He is not to blame for simply because they have a false impression of Who God really is.

Perhaps the most infamous false impression the people of God have about the Person of God is...

"God brings storms in your life to bring you closer to Him."

This statement is so not biblical, yet many believers swear by it. Whenever something is going wrong, either God has sent this storm to bring us closer to Him or *"The devil is busy"*.

Why can't people just assume personal responsibility for their actions or inactions? God is very clear about what happens when we don't follow ALL the instructions (Deuteronomy 28:15-29). Yes, the devil is busy but why can't people just accept that *sometimes* we stir up life's storms through our own disobedience? Our disobedience severs our divine connection with God and when we are disconnected from the Power Source, we give the enemy free reign over our lives.

We may not want to accept it but again, the law of seedtime and harvest operates today with the same precision and power as when God first instituted it. Every seed we sow *will* reap a harvest (and bad seeds seem to harvest more rapidly at the most inopportune time).

What happens is God sometimes *uses* these storms to bring us closer to Him but I can say with boldness and confidence that He *never sends* storms in our life for *any* reason whatsoever.

> **"The Lord is gracious and full of compassion, slow to anger and abounding in mercy and lovingkindness. The Lord is good to all, and His tender mercies are over all His works [the entirety of things created]."**
> **Psalm 145:8-9 AMP**

> **"Every good gift and every perfect gift is from above, and cometh down from the Father of lights, with whom is no variableness, neither shadow of turning."**
> **James 1:17**

So many people negate the Old Testament until they need to validate their premise about God's wrath in their life. Well, I'm using both the Old and New Testament to validate His character as a loving Father who is gracious and merciful toward His children.

And I THANK GOD FOR JESUS because Christ has redeemed us from the curse of the law and it is because of Jesus that we experience the fullness of our Father's grace and mercy and that we have been blessed to be a blessing.

Let the people of God say…

I AM BLESSED TO BE A BLESSING!

But we can't be a blessing to others if *we* don't have enough or only have just enough for our four and no more.

Yes, *in Christ*, God has *already* given us everything we need to live a godly life that is pleasing to Him but we have to abide by the "IF stips"…

"What is an 'IF stip'?" you ask.

An "IF stip" is a conditional statement: IF this, THEN that. IF this stipulation is met, the statement following "THEN" is executed.

The Word of God is full of "IF" stips or what I like to call *"the provision to the provision"* or *"the stipulated condition to the activity of providing."*

Matthew 6:33 is one of many "IF stips" found in the Word.

[IF] we seek (aim at and strive after) the Kingdom of God first of all…above all else and His righteousness (His way of doing & being right)
[THEN] He will give us everything we need.

What's already been given to us and what's rightfully ours will only manifest in our life when we comply with the "IF stip". We can't just skip the "stip" and expect God to be in compliance. It doesn't work that way.

I get a little perturbed when I hear believers justify their lack by lying on God.

"Oh no, she didn't just say that!"

Oh YES, I did just say it and not to be offensive…just keepin' it real. That's exactly what some believers are doing…*lying on God*…to justify their lack.

In Step One, we discussed the first white lie people tell on God to justify their situation…*"God is getting ready to…"* whatever. Seriously, why does God have to *get ready* to do anything? That doesn't even make sense.

In the beginning, did God say, "Let us *get ready* to create light"? NO. He said, *"Let there be light"* and what? *"There was light."* Did He say, "Let us *get ready* to make man in our image"? NO. He said, *"Let us make man in our image"* and what? *"God created man in His own image, in the image of God created He him; Male and female created He them."* (Genesis 1:27)

SIDEBAR: As I was typing this scripture, I began wondering why this statement was repeated three times. There is significance to everything in the Word. The Holy Spirit quickly revealed to me that the repetition represents "US", the Trinity – Father, Son and Holy Spirit.

STEP BACK: So why, pray tell, would God need to *get ready* to do anything in our life? Nothing He would be getting ready to do would measure up in stature to what He's already done since the beginning of time.

I'm just saying…

Another common "white lie" people tell on God to justify their situation has to do with the favor of God.

> *"Well, I may not have much money but what I do have is the favor of God. I really don't need money because God's favor is all I need."*

Without reservation, I wholeheartedly agree that the favor of God is independent and incomparable. Here's the problem I have with this out of line thinking – it's so heavenly minded that it's no earthly good. Now before you get all bent out of shape, I am aware that the Word admonishes us to set our minds on things above and not on earthly things (Colossians 3:2).

However, let me point out the fact that the author of Colossians 3:2 and the author of Romans 12:2 are one and the same, the Apostle Paul (by inspiration of the Holy Spirit). Based on the context and content of both passages of scripture, it is my belief that Colossians 3:2 reinforces Romans 12:2 (NLT).

> **"Don't copy the behavior and customs of this world, but let God transform you into a new person by changing the way you think."**

When we let God transform our carnal, earthly thinking to be more spiritual, more focused on the things of God, our minds will be set on things above and not so much on earthly things. But with this transformation comes the realization that it is not God's intention for us to use our status as citizens of the Kingdom as justification for non-compliance with the laws of this land (unless they violate *His* laws) because His favor is on our life.

I recently heard the story of a state patrol officer, who stopped for coffee and donuts and parked his cruiser in a handicap parking space even though he wasn't handicap and although there were several parking spaces in the area. When questioned about his choice by a concerned citizen, this officer got angry, proceeded to reprimand and threaten to arrest this man.

This officer used his status in law enforcement to bend the rules because clearly, he thought he was *above the law*.

We are not of this world but we are in this world and while we are in this world, our heavenly citizenship does not give us carte blanche to circumvent or ignore the realities of living life in this world.

> **"Render to all men their dues. [Pay] taxes to whom taxes are due, revenue to whom revenue is due, respect to whom respect is due, and honor to whom honor is due."**
>
> **Romans 13:7 AMP**

You can't, after you max out all your credit cards, decide that because the favor of God is on your life that you don't have to pay the bills. You can't spend the mortgage money on a new pair of Manolo Blahniks or a Versace suit for Sunday morning service and get up with a straight face and testify, *"I may not have money to pay my mortgage but I'm not worried 'cause I know the favor of God is on my life."*

NO...NO...NO!

Let the people of God say...

"DO THE RIGHT THING!!

As born-again believers, we know that we are already recipients of God's unmerited favor...it's His gift to us (Ephesians 2:8). In our everyday living, God continues to work His favor in our life in diverse ways but people we gotta do the right thing.

And when we do, the favor of God will flow freely in our life. God may decide to favor some of His children with miracle debt cancellation. Because of our obedience to His mandate of tithing and giving, He may place it on someone's heart somewhere to pay off all our debt in full. We may never know who made the payment but we will always know *why* they made the payment.

Or He may decide to favor us with miracle debt reduction. He may place it on someone's heart in the accounts receivable department to review our account with a fine tooth comb, who realizes that we don't even owe the amount they thought we owed.

God's favor always flows freely in our life...when we do the right thing. In the meantime, we can't just neglect our responsibilities on the premise that the favor of God is on our life.

Let the people of God say...

"JUST DO THE RIGHT THING!!"

God is omniscient. He knows everything there is to know about everything and everyone. He knows that money is the primary medium of exchange in our society. As such, He knows that money is necessary for our survival on this earth.

Why else would He give us power to get wealth?

Although Deuteronomy 8:18 has sometimes been misinterpreted to mean God *gives* us wealth, what it *says* is God *gives us power* to produce wealth.

Ephesians 3:20 tells us that *according to* how *we* work *the power He's given us*, He is able to do exceeding abundantly above all that we ask or think. That can only mean that He is *unable* to do exceeding abundantly above all that we ask or think if we don't work the power He's given us. The ball is in our court.

Let the people of God say...

"I'VE GOT THE POWER!!"

When believers make statements like the ones above, in essence, what they're telling God is that they expect Him to do *His* part – *exceeding abundantly above all that they ask or think* – without expecting to have to do their part – *working the power that He's given them*.

Again, this is the major reason there are so many believers sitting in the waiting room, waiting for God to do *something else* while they justify their negligence by making counterfeit confessions.

People of God, our life should be a reflection of Who we represent – Whose Team we're on.

Let me share a simple example. At the time of this writing, the NBA finals between the LA Lakers and the Boston Celtics are airing. Most avid basketball fans are pretty familiar with the uniforms of the teams in the NBA. The Lakers' uniform is purple and gold. The Celtics' uniform is green and white.

Do you think for one minute that a Lakers team player would come out on the court dressed in green and white or that a Celtics team player would come out on the court in purple and gold?

Absolutely not! There would be a mutiny on the court. Each respective team player is expected to wear the uniform that reflects the team they represent.

Likewise, we are on Team Kingdom and yes, the favor of God is on our life. If we're walking around saying the favor of God is on our life, then folk should be seeing the favor of God in our life. We should be wearing the "uniform" of the team we represent.

> *Our uniform should have a double "B" for BLESSED BELIEVER!!*

How can we effectively minister about the abundant blessings of God to broke folk if, based on our representation, it looks like we serve a God Who makes a whole lot of promises that He doesn't keep?

Abundance, not lack, is evidence of God's favor on our life; love, not hate, is evidence of God's favor on our life; peace, not confusion is evidence of God's favor on our life; faith, not fear is evidence of God's favor on our life.

Let me tell you something: I don't believe that justifying lack by saying the favor of God is on our life is at all favorable to God. It actually gives Him a bad rep. The favor of God is only manifested in our life when we study the Book and play by the rules.

Let the people of God say...

"I JUST GOTTA DO THE RIGHT THING!!"

Society has much to say about blessed believers that are walking in God's favor. I say, let them have their say because it really doesn't matter in the least what society is says. The only thing that *really* matters is what God says.

Let's talk about the favor of God on Jesus' life for a minute.

While on earth, Jesus obeyed and operated within the confines of the laws and customs of the land, provided they were not in violation of the laws of God. In Matthew 17:24-27 we find Jesus, although the favor of God was on His life, submitting to human authority…specifically with regard to money.

As was customary in the Jewish faith, every male, age twenty and older, was required to pay an annual religious tax called the *Shekalim* in his own province or at the Temple in Jerusalem. This temple tax, which originated in Exodus 30:11-16 as payment for atonement, was used for the preservation of the Temple.

It was also customary, or so it seems, for the religious leaders of Jesus' time to look for any opportunity they could find to try and trip Jesus up. This particular incident was no different.

> **"After Jesus and his disciples arrived in Capernaum, the collectors of the two-drachma tax came to Peter and asked, 'Doesn't your teacher pay the temple tax?' 'Yes, he does,' he replied. When Peter came into the house, Jesus was the first to speak. 'What do you think, Simon?' he asked. 'From whom do the kings of the earth collect duty and taxes—from their own sons or from others?' 'From others,' Peter answered. 'Then the sons are exempt,' Jesus said to him."**
>
> **Matthew 17:24-26 NIV**

Jesus was the King's Son. The Temple was His Father's house and He was greater than the Temple (Matthew 12:6). Being the sinless Son of the King, Jesus was really under no obligation to pay this temple tax.

What I love about Jesus is how diplomatically He made His point. Voluntarily, in His humanity and with the greatest humility, Jesus made provision for Peter to get the money that not only paid His own temple tax, but paid Peter's temple tax as well…

"…so that we may not offend them."

This payment not only set the precedent for the premium price of atonement Jesus was about to pay for the sins of the world but it was a graphic demonstration of God's intention for His people to be blessed and be a blessing.

So in spite of what some may believe and/or say, there is nothing wrong with wanting money; there is nothing wrong with having money and there is nothing wrong with enjoying the money we have.

There *is* something wrong when worshipping cash takes precedence over worshipping Christ.

> **"No one can serve two masters. For you will hate one and love the other; you will be devoted to one and despise the other. You cannot serve both God and money."**
>
> **Matthew 6:24 NLT**

When we love God more than we love the world, we won't be conformed to the world. When we love the world more than we love God, we won't be transformed by the Word and it will cost us our life.

Jesus says in John 12:25…

> **"Those who love their life in this world will lose it. Those who care nothing for their life in this world will keep it for eternity."**

People who give up their faith for the love of money love their life in this world more than they love God and in the end, it *will* cost them much more than they expected to pay in every way.

This is the mindset Paul is speaking about in 1 Timothy 6…a maniacal mind motivated by money.

People with messed up mindsets spin webs of selfishness and self-sufficiency. Paul warns these rich people *"not to be proud or to trust in wealth that is so easily lost"* (1 Timothy 6:17 CEV).

As we evaluate the volatile situation in our world today, we see that God's Word, once again, is proven to be true. We see how this economic earthquake has shaken this feeble foundation of pride, greed and misplaced trust to the core. We have seen first hand how funds invested heavily in this world system and everything tied into these funds – jobs, homes, cars – can be here today…gone today.

The bottom of the basket has fallen out, Humpty Dumpty has had a great fall and all the king's horses and all the king's men are desperately trying to pick up the pieces and put Humpty back together again.

But if God ain't in it, all the king's horses and all the king's men that labor, labor in vain (Psalm 127:1).

> **"It is better to trust in the LORD than to put confidence in man."**
>
> **Psalm 118:8**

Paul echoes this wisdom…

> **"Their trust should be in God, who richly gives us all we need for our enjoyment."**
>
> **1 Timothy 6:17 NIV**

Then there are those believers who are on the receiving end but are arrogantly walking in their "Promised Land". They placed their trust in the Giver and received the gifts but now they've "misplaced" their trust more in the gifts than the Giver. They forget to remember that it **ALL** belongs to God...

> **"The earth is the Lord's, and everything in it. The world and all its people belong to him."**
>
> **Psalm 24:1 NLT**

...and it **ALL** comes from God...

> **"But remember the LORD your God, for it is he who gives you the ability to produce wealth…"**
>
> **Deuteronomy 8:18 NIV**

Deuteronomy 7:17 (CEV) warns us, *"When you become successful, don't say, 'I'm rich, and I've earned it all myself.'"* This passage of scripture is as applicable to the rich and famous as it is to the redeemed and favored.

As our Chief Financial Officer, we are required to trust God and obey His directives concerning how we manage what He has entrusted us with. God is no respecter of persons; He is a respecter of trust and obedience.

> **"Instruct them to do as many good deeds as they can and to help everyone. Remind the rich to be generous and share what they have. This will lay a solid foundation for the future, so that they will know what true life is like."**
>
> **1 Timothy 6:18 CEV**

If we don't master our mind concerning our money, our money will master our mind.

So why are we so fixated on putting all our eggs in this earthly basket? The most expensive, exquisite earthly treasures that money can buy in no way compare to what God has in store for those of us who store our treasures in the Kingdom of Heaven.

How do we store our treasures in the Kingdom of Heaven?

Regardless of the misapplication that is occurring and the resulting mistrust that has occurred in the body of Christ, God requires us to honor Him with our first and our best and trust Him with the rest (Proverbs 3:9, Malachi 3:10).

We store treasure in Heaven when we make taking care of Kingdom business our priority. The Ministry of Giving into Kingdom business is a privilege, not an obligation. A mastered mind knows that when we take care of God's ten, our ninety goes long.

Any genuine investment made in Kingdom business is a sound investment that will yield an unprecedented return.

But it starts with our heart. If we don't master our mind to the reality that He is the Master of our money, we will never be able to master our money.

God desires to do exceedingly and abundantly more than we might ask or think or even imagine in our life. He wants to give us the desires of our heart – our recreated newborn heart not a selfish, carnal heart.

The desires of our recreated newborn heart reflect our renewed mastered mind. When we are divinely connected through an intimate One-on-one relationship with God, there is a priority shift from solely seeking financial riches to attaining spiritual riches.

The desires of a selfish, carnal heart are to simply satisfy our fleshly cravings. This heart is much more susceptible to succumb to the ambush of temptations that has been set for its destruction because a divine connection has never been established or if it was established, has been severed.

A severed or short-circuited connection is the primary reason people are deceived and relinquish their faith in God for the love of money.

Securing our connection is the primary route believers must take if we are to dispel the deceptive data and release our faith that God's Master Plan **IS** for us to live an abundant life – a life that overflows with His goodness.

David says in Psalm 27:13 (AMP)...

"[What, what would have become of me] *had I not believed* **that I would see the Lord's goodness in the land of the living!"**

It's not hard to see what has become of believers who don't believe that God's Master Plan **IS** for us to live an abundant life that overflows with His goodness.

- They are living in crisis
  ...when our calling is *to live in Christ*!
- They are living in fear...
  ...when our calling is *to live by faith*.
- They are living impoverished...
  ...when our calling is *to live empowered*.

Believers who don't believe are believers who won't receive because they are believers who can't conceive God's Master Plan in their spirit. We won't "get it" until we "get it".

I'm here to let you know that it's never too late to be and do what God has called us to be and do. No matter what our current situation is, believers need only believe that God is Who He says He is and that He has done what He said He did.

"Anything is possible if a person believes."

What's interesting about Mark 9:23 (NLT) is it is unbiased. It works however we work it. It works for whatever we believe. If we believe God's Word, we will experience an overflow of promises; if we believe Satan's word, we will experience an overflow of problems.

Believers who have been shaken and stirred by this economic earthquake have chosen to believe the deceptive data that has been disseminated by Satan.

Believers who stand solid and sure are not shaken by this economic earthquake because we believe the report of the Lord and we know that we have not been forsaken (Psalm 37:25).

That's why it's ultra important that we stay connected to the Power Source so we can clearly hear what God has to say, believe what He has to say and do what He says to do so we can receive what He says is ours.

It's sad to see how deceptive data has conditioned so many believers to trust in the wisdom of this world more than they trust in the wisdom of God. Don't you know that the wisdom of this world is foolishness in God's sight (1 Corinthians 3:19 NIV)?

As we assess this mess, it's plain to see that the wisdom of the world is foolish and the wisdom of God is flawless.

Unless you are a born-again, Spirit-filled, Spirit-led believer, everything I've shared in this book will sound foolish to you because the carnal natural mind cannot receive the pure spiritual things of God. Even so, know this: the most foolish plan of God is wiser than the wisest plan of men (1 Corinthians 3:25).

We will always come out on top when we operate in accordance with God's ordinances no matter how foolish they look to man because God uses things that the world considers foolish in order to shame those who think they are wise...*that no flesh should glory in His presence.* (1 Corinthians 1:27-29).

We must dismantle and dismiss the deceptive data that has been ingrained in our brain so we can walk in our destiny of dominion and live out God's divine design for our life…in this life.

Dynamic Duo

If living in the "overflow" IS God's Master Plan for His people, why aren't all God's people living in the "overflow"?

We've already determined that one reason believers are not living in the overflow is they've been duped by the dissemination of deceptive data. There are a number of other reasons why believers are not living in the overflow but I venture to examine one reason that possibly serves as the basis for every other reason.

Let's call it T²O...the dynamic duo.

There's an old hymn that says..."*Trust and obey for there's no other way to be happy in Jesus but to trust and obey.*"

> *There is no other way.*
> *ALL roads lead to trust and obedience!*

Trust and obedience, part one of the dynamic duo, are the keys that unlock the vault of our inheritance to God's promises.

> **"If you are willing and obedient, you will eat the best from the land."**
> Isaiah 1:19 NIV

The main reason not all God's people are living in the overflow is because not all God's people trust God.

That may be a hard pill to swallow but it's the truth anyhow.

Most believers don't believe or trust God like we should. Yes, believers are quick to confess *"I believe God"* but our actions speak so much louder than our confession.

We know that God can be trusted (or at least we should) but when we get between that rock and that hard place what we say and what we do are on the opposite sides of the fence.

We don't trust God like we should because we don't know God like we should. Sure, we may believe *in* God and know *of* Him but we don't *really believe* the God we believe in and we don't *really know* the God we know of. If we really believe God is Who He says He is, we would know that He can be trusted and we would have no problem trusting Him.

We can never really believe God or trust in God until we really get to know God. So many believers believe that developing an intimate relationship with God is so elusive but developing an intimate relationship with God is pretty much the same as developing an intimate relationship with anyone else.

The more quality time we invest with an individual, the better we get to know that individual; the better we get to know that individual, the more intimate our relationship with them becomes. The more intimate our relationship with that individual, the higher the trust factor.

> *Our relationship with God is THE most important relationship in our life.*

That's the difference between our relationship with God and all other relationships. Because God is the Relationship Manager, our relationship with Him is foundational. The success of every relationship we encounter in life hinges on the success of our relationship with God. Yet, we spend the least amount of time developing an intimate relationship with Him.

Down through the years, our investment strategy has been to heavily invest our time in developing our natural relationships with our family and friends and rightfully so. Those relationships do require our time and attention.

However, because we've modestly invested time and attention in developing our spiritual relationship with our Creator and Father, it has yielded a spiritual deficiency that has ultimately caused our natural relationships to suffer significantly – divorce among believers is at an all time high, families are dysfunctional, there is discord in our churches, our communities are in disarray and our nation is discombobulated.

Our time investment in the things of this world has produced misplaced trust. We trust more in people and professions and possessions and it isn't until all hell breaks loose, that we decide to trust God, as our last resort.

> **"It is better to trust in the LORD than to put confidence in man."**
>
> **Psalm 118:8**

We don't even need to spend so much time learning to trust other people because even with all that time spent, there's still no "money back guarantee" that they can be trusted. When we invest quality time establishing an intimate relationship with God, our return on investment is like no other. As we learn to trust Him completely, He will show us everything we need to know about the people we encounter.

Hear the Word of the LORD, ye His saints...

> **"My people are destroyed because they don't know me."**
>
> **Hosea 4:6 NLT**

By His divine power, God has given us everything we need for living a godly life. 2 Peter 1:3 (NLT) tells us that we receive all of this by *getting to know Him.*

How can we ever expect to get to know Him if we don't invest quality time establishing an intimate relationship with Him? How can we ever expect to get to know Him if we don't spend time in His presence (and not just for His presents)? How can we ever expect to get to know Him if we don't abide by Joshua 1:8 and Matthew 6:33?

So because we don't really know God like we should, we don't trust God like we should. Practically speaking, how much trust do you have in people you don't really know? And because we don't trust God like we should, we don't obey Him.

It is expedient that we be obedient.

Disobedience severs our divine connection to the Power Source. A severed connection means "ACCESS DENIED" to the life by divine design God has in mind.

Just like the children of Israel, the people of God have been wandering through the wilderness for years on a journey that was never intended to be this long because we refuse to trust God implicitly and obey Him immediately.

David had an intimate relationship with God. God called him *"a man after mine own heart."* David knew who God was…

> **"I will say of the Lord, He is my refuge and my fortress: my God;** *in Him will I trust.***"**
> **Psalm 91:2**

Not only did David trust God, he taught his son, Solomon to trust God (Proverbs 3:5-6 AMP)…

> **"Lean on, trust in, and be confident in the Lord with all your heart and mind and do not rely on your own insight or understanding. In all your ways know, recognize, and acknowledge Him, and He will direct and make straight and plain your paths."**

We can't *"lean on, trust in and be confident in"* God for guidance and direction until we *"know, recognize and acknowledge"* Him as our Spiritual Navigator.

Our lack of knowledge, trust and obedience has us staggering when we should swaggering at God's promises; when we, like David, should be boasting about the goodness of God in our lives and inviting others to experience His goodness.

> **"O taste and see that the LORD is good:** ***blessed is the man that trusteth in him."***
> **Psalm 34:8**

But how can we invite others to experience God's goodness when, because of our lack of knowledge, trust and obedience, we've yet to experience the fullness thereof?

How can we effectively minister to a sick man that Jesus is a healer if we're sick in our spirit, soul and body? How can we effectively minister to a broke man that Jesus is a provider if we're living from paycheck to paycheck, trying to make ends meet?

> *Before we can share God,*
> *our lives should be showing God.*

Before we can show Him, we've got to know Him.

Our obedience to God's Word and our vulnerability to Satan's lies are both based on our trust in God's Word which is based on our knowledge of God.

Willingly trusting and obeying God positions us to experience the abundant life of power, peace and prosperity that God designed for us.

Willingly trusting and obeying God conditions our mind to the things of God and a renewed mind dominated by the Spirit seeks God's way of doing and being right...*above all else.*

Simply put, if every believer wants to live in the overflow, we must make it our business to know God, to trust God and to obey God.

> **"Obey me, and I will be your God, and you will be my people.** *Do everything as I say, and all will be well!"*
>
> **Jeremiah 7:23 NLT**

The word "overflow" is clearly a compound word comprised of the words "over" and "flow". One definition of the word "flow" is *"to proceed continuously and smoothly"*. "Over" can be used synonymously with the word "surplus" and a surplus is *"something that remains above what is used or needed."*

Would it be reasonable to presume that in order to live in the overflow or *above* the flow, one must first live *in* the flow?

Would it then be reasonable to presume that not all God's people are living in the overflow because not all God's people are living *in the flow*– that is, *GOD's flow*?

The prerequisite to living in John 10:10 overflow is living in "Matthew 6:33 flow" which **IS** God's flow. It is impossible to live in John 10:10 overflow unless we are first living in Matthew 6:33 flow. It is also impossible to live in "3 John 2 prosperity" unless we are first living in Matthew 6:33 flow.

> **"Seek the Kingdom of God** *above all else*, **and live righteously, and he will give you everything you need."**
>
> **Matthew 6:33 NLT**

The universal theme in John 10:10, 3 John 2 and Matthew 6:33 is that *above all things*…it is the will of God for His children to live an abundant life of power, peace and prosperity – spirit, soul and body. But *God's will* can only be fulfilled when we seek *God's way* of doing and being right…*above all else*.

Living *in God's flow* means living *in Christ*. The abundant life spoken of *by Christ* in John 10:10 can only be found *in Christ*.

Living *in God's flow* means that we trust God implicitly and obey Him immediately.

Let the people of God say...

"There Is No Other Way."

People of God, when we consistently live *in God's flow*, seeking His way of doing and being right, we can expect a blizzard of blessings to blanket every area of our life.

When we consistently live in the world's flow, we can expect to live in a series of crises. Believers who are living in crisis have disregarded Paul's directive in Romans 12:2 and have become comfortably acclimated to the world's "go with the flow" mentality. They maintain a facade of godliness to conceal the real deal but they deny, not rely on the genuine Power that is available to them to live successfully *in God's flow*.

Many believers are so entangled and engrossed in the ways of the world that they have become entrapped and ensnared by the wiles of the world. Some believers have become so well-adjusted to the culture of this world that, in these last days, it is increasingly difficult to tell the difference between a born-again believer – an individual who has voiced their choice to receive and live a new life *in Christ* – and a nonbeliever – an individual who has no belief or faith in God.

Believers have become chameleons – blending in when we should be standing out.

I recently read a statement that said God made His children in such a way that when the people of the world are sitting, we would be standing; when the world is standing, we would stand out; when the world stands out, we would be outstanding and when the devil dares the world to be outstanding, we would be the standards to be used!

This malignant merger, coupled with identity theft, has had an adverse effect on believers that has drastically altered the dynamics of this scenario and has neutralized our effectiveness.

Going with the world's flow has many believers drifting downstream in the strong negative flow of this world right with nonbelievers – thinking negatively, speaking negatively and spending negatively – and it totally goes against the grain of our calling *in Christ...*

> **"Let me tell you why you are here. You're here to be salt-seasoning that brings out the God-flavors of this earth. If you lose your saltiness, how will people taste godliness? ... Here's another way to put it: You're here to be light, bringing out the God-colors in the world."**
> **Matthew 5:13-14 MSG**

God has called us to be beacons of light in this dark world. God has called us to add godly flavor to a world of fabricated flamboyance. The only way we can do this effectively is by living in John 10:10 overflow. But before we can live in John 10:10 overflow, we must adopt and adhere to Matthew 6:33 flow and cease to admire and accept the "go with the flow" mentality of the world.

This "Master Plan" is a spiritual fitness program designed to properly prepare us and securely position us *in God's flow* so that the reality of John 10:10 overflow can be *our* reality.

Step Three is considerably shorter than Steps One and Two because financial prosperity is inspired by and acquired through spiritual prosperity. The focal point of Steps One and Two is attaining spiritual prosperity.

We can't even get to Step Three: Master Your Money without getting through Steps One and Two.

Step One: Master Your Mind involves fine-tuning our reception so we can clearly recognize the voice of the Holy Spirit and hear <u>and</u> heed His guidance concerning every area of our life including our fiscal responsibility. During Step One as we get to intimately know God, we come to the realization that the Ministry of Finance has absolutely nothing to do with God *needing "our" money*. God doesn't need our money.

God does need us to trust and obey Him.

Matthew 6:33 sets the tone for the ordinances in the Ministry of Finance that require our trust and obedience. If we don't *seek God's way of doing and being right*, we won't likely obey His mandate concerning part two of T²O – tithes and offering.

Step Two: Master Your Mouth involves fine-tuning our articulation to clearly speak "with" the voice of the Holy Spirit concerning every area of our life including finance. During Step Two, as we get to intimately know God, we come to the realization that our having has a lot to do with our saying.

It never ceases to amaze me how lightly we take God's commands including, but not limited to, the area of finances, when the consequences are so weighty. These commands are direct orders; not suggestions.

Military discipline is built on the foundation of obedience to orders. When a direct order is issued, it is expected that the order be executed without hesitation or question. Military members who fail to comply with the lawful orders of their superiors risk serious consequences. It is a crime to willfully disobey a direct order.

Can you see how although they would never openly admit it, in many ways the world patterns itself after the powerful principles found in the Word of God?

Christian discipline is built on the foundation of obedience to God's orders. God expects us to execute His orders without hesitation or question. Failure to comply with His orders has produced serious consequences in our life.

> **"…keep the words of this covenant and do them, that you may deal wisely and prosper in all that you do."**
> **Deuteronomy 29:9 AMP**

If we refuse to obey the voice of God, we will be destroyed (Deuteronomy 8:20).

The Master Design: Step Three

The dilemma for most folk is God's Word is a minority – not a priority in their life. But if we want God's promises to prevail in our life so that we can live an abundant life of power, peace and prosperity, we need to make His Word our number one priority.

Malachi 3:9-10 (AMP) is the quintessential Old Testament passage of scripture that speaks directly to the divine connection between tithing and the overflow...

> **"Bring all the tithes (the whole tenth of your income) into the storehouse, that there may be food in My house, and prove Me now by it, says the Lord of hosts, if I will not open the windows of heaven for you and pour you out a blessing,** *that there shall not be room enough to receive it.*"

The "IF stip" in a nutshell in Malachi 3:10 is IF we make sure there is food in God's House THEN God will make sure there's food in ours. I particularly like the double emphasis He puts on getting our blessing to us. He's going to open and pour – not crack and sprinkle – our blessings out the windows of Heaven until our cup runs over!

Let the people of God say...

"Sounds Like Overflow To Me!"

Again, if we are not living in Matthew 6:33 flow, our hearts will not be primed to honor Him with the ten and trust Him with the ninety.

Don't you find it interesting that the one passage of scripture in the Word where the Lord challenges us to put Him to the test has to do with finances?

Why do you think that is?

First, realize that tithing is not simply a money issue; tithing is a covenant issue. Some New Covenant believers don't believe tithing is necessary since it was an Old Covenant command and is not specifically mentioned under the New Covenant.

As we all know from personal experience, when it comes to money, people start acting funny.

The reason most believers act funny when it comes to "their" money is because they are operating outside Matthew 6:33 flow. Their minds have not been renewed to God's way of doing and being right and so their thinkin' is stinkin' when it comes to givin'.

The purpose of the tithe under the Old Covenant was to meet the financial needs of ministry. Under the New Covenant, there are still financial needs that must be met in ministry. What has happened is people are holding back their tithe because of the misapplication of finances and mistrust running rampant in the body of Christ.

I'm not going to get too deep into this because my purpose is not to incite a riot over the issue of tithing but I will say this…if we would get *in God's flow* and seek His way of doing and being right, if we would seek to fully comprehend the concept of covenant, the potency of our covenant with God and to live more covenant-conscious, tithing would be perceived as a blessing and a privilege, not a legalistic burden.

Our mere ten percent can never repay God for what He's done for us *in Christ* to ratify this New Covenant that is established on *better* promises. That, in and of itself, should be sufficient enough for us to cheerfully give.

How much sense does it even make for us to squabble over something God designed to communicate His blessings to His people?

When you stop to think about it, it's nothing more than another deliberate distraction designed to keep from us what God has already promised to us.

Either you're gonna do it or you're not. Just stop fighting about it and do whatever you decide to do.

Finances are a necessity to live successfully in this life. You can say what you want but you can do more with money than you can without it. That's just the reality of it. I recently heard a minister say on a radio advertisement, *"You don't need a lot of money to do what God wants you to do."*

It's this messed up mindset that has the people of God living beneath their privilege. Although Paul doesn't specifically mention tithing in the New Testament, he does extensive teaching on the topic of fiscal responsibility as it pertains to Kingdom business.

It takes money to run Kingdom business just like it takes money to run any other business. IF we take care of Kingdom business THEN God will take care of our business.

The financial ordinances God has set in place grant us unlimited access to His infinite riches in glory *in Christ* to do everything He wants us to do.

Although it appears that the challenge in Malachi 3:9-10 is designed to show us what God is capable of doing, this challenge is really designed to show God what *we* are capable of doing; if we are capable of trusting Him enough to obey Him.

Malachi 3:10 establishes the word in Proverbs 3:9-10 (AMP)…

> **"Honor the Lord with your capital and sufficiency [from righteous labors] and with the firstfruits of all your income; So shall your storage places be *filled with plenty*, and your vats shall *be overflowing* with new wine."**

Let the people of God say…

"SOUNDS LIKE OVERFLOW TO ME!"

Tithing is an honor. God says the tithe is holy (Leviticus 27:30). We honor God when we show Him that we trust Him and obey Him with the crème de la crème from our legitimate business enterprises. God honors our trust and obedience by blessing us with an avalanche of abundance.

> *The truth is we can't afford NOT to give.*

Luke 6:38 (NLT), a well-known, often recited promise says...

> **"Give, and you will receive. Your gift will return to you in full—pressed down, shaken together to make room for more, *running over*, and poured into your lap."**

Everybody loves to hear and recite everything before the second period in Luke 6:38 but you don't hear too much recitation about anything after that period...

> **"The amount you give will determine the amount you get back."**

The law of seedtime and harvest is still in full effect. 2 Corinthians 9:6 (AMP) corroborates Luke 6:38...

> **"[Remember] this: he who sows sparingly and grudgingly will also reap sparingly and grudgingly, and he who *sows generously* [that blessings may come to someone] will also *reap generously* and with blessings."**

The body of Christ today does not honor God in our giving because we are not operating *in God's flow*. And because we are not operating *in God's flow*, this economic earthquake has shaken so many believers to the core that they truly believe they can't afford to give.

Then there are the socially-acceptable messages being preached that have diluted and polluted the prosperity message and left believers cutting off their nose to spite their face.

The determining factor in our giving is whether we allow fear to override our faith. If we have not mastered our mind concerning money, chances are fear will override our faith. If we are not trusting God as we should, fear will override our faith.

- When fear overrides our faith, we give God what's left...not what's right.

- When fear overrides our faith, we make excuses about why we can't give as much as we'd like to.

- When fear overrides our faith, we mumble and grumble about how many cars the Pastor and his wife and kids have and what a big house they live in.

- When fear overrides our faith, we increase our vulnerability to the attacks of the enemy...in every area of our life, not just our finances.

- When fear overrides our faith, we inhibit God's ability to intervene on our behalf because God is a respecter and a responder of faith, not fear.

Listen, people, God doesn't require us to give because He needs what we have – God *does not* need our money – He requires us to give because *we* need what *He* has. He's not trying to take something from us; He's trying to get something to us.

Giving paves the way for God to release His choice blessings in our life. When we seek His way of doing and being right...

> "**...God will generously provide all you need. Then you will always have everything you need and *plenty left over to share with others.*"**
>
> **2 Corinthians 9:8 NLT**

There's an old song that says, *"You can't beat God giving, no matter how you try."* Why? There is no deficiency in Heaven's economy – only sufficiency.

Let the people of God say…

"I REFUSE TO LET FEAR INTERFERE WITH MY FAITH!"

The problem with the prosperity message in the body of Christ as it is being taught is it depicts financial breakthrough as a game of chance. As I mentioned earlier, the socially-acceptable messages that are being preached encourage the unscriptural notion of "buying a breakthrough".

I've seen believers at conferences make their way to the stage to throw their money at the feet of the ministers of God.

This scene kindles a mental picture in my mind of gamblers playing craps, a game of chance, on the street corner. There may be a logical explanation for this behavior but I have yet to find a biblical one.

Biblically, it is reminiscent of the scene in Matthew 21 where Jesus, upon entering the Temple, found unsavory undertakings and cleared the temple with righteous indignation because these businessmen had turned His House of Prayer into a den of thieves.

I've seen Ministers invite believers to line up in the $500, $100, $50 or $10 line with the assurance that this offering will yield a financial breakthrough "in seven days". The bigger the offering – the bigger the breakthrough.

Reluctantly, in response to the pressure, people get on these lines and put in the money for their gas bill or light bill and seven days later, they're sitting in a cold, dark house. They put in their last, out of fear, expecting this financial breakthrough that the man of God has promised. Our offering should be voluntary, not coerced.

Now we all know that God can do anything and everything is possible for him that believes but God won't decrease His response time because of our desperation. God responds to our trust in His Word and our obedience to His Word. Besides that, God loves a cheerful, not fearful giver. He is motivated to move on our behalf if our motives are pure, not polluted.

It's no wonder the prosperity message has come under scrutiny and is being ridiculed. It's no wonder believers believe that Ministers preaching "this" prosperity message are "Pimpin' the People."

There's an old proverb that says, *"One bad apple spoils the whole barrel"*. Of course, we know that not everyone in the barrel is spoiled but perception is reality. The world believes what it sees and what the world sees is a bunch of broke folk giving away money to preachers who are styling and profiling while their church members are busted and disgusted.

It's a matter of making a quality decision whether to honor God with our tithes and offering so that the windows of heaven can open wide and our storage places can be *filled with plenty* until they *overflow*.

Financial breakthrough is a matter of choice.

As ridiculous as it may sound to some of God's people, there are many of God's people who believe the Word, are doing what the Word says to do and are receiving what the Word promised they would receive.

In his book, *"Increase God's Way"*, Jerry Savelle says "there is absolutely no way that you can walk with God, keep His covenant and not experience financial increase."

Until we receive true knowledge and understanding about the Ministry of Giving, the spirit in which we give will impede our ability to receive all that God has for us.

Until we master our mind to realize that God needs our obedience more than He needs our money, our hearts won't be primed to honor Him in our giving.

> **"You must each decide in your heart how much to give. And don't give reluctantly or in response to pressure.** *'For God loves a person who gives cheerfully.'"*
>
> 2 Corinthians 9:7 NLT

A cheerful giver has a renewed mind and a regenerated attitude about God and money because a cheerful giver has an intimate One-on-one relationship with God.

A renewed mind has received revelation that it **ALL** belongs to God anyway and it is He Who gives us power to produce wealth.

A renewed mind has come to the realization that money is not evil, it's essential…not just for us to mind our own business but to also mind Kingdom business.

The first of two familiar stories that come to mind that demonstrate that God is big on overflow is the story of the widow's oil. This multifaceted story, found in 2 Kings 4:1-7, has quite a few significant lessons to be learned but my emphasis, for all intents and purposes, is the Power that is released when we give cheerfully…even in the midst of challenging circumstances.

As the story unfolds, the widow of one of Elisha's servants approaches the Prophet in dire straits. Her husband, who was a devote man of God, had recently passed away, leaving behind a significant amount of debt.

I say it was a "significant" amount because the collector of the debt intended to collect on his debt by taking this man's two sons as slaves to work off this debt.

That may appear to be severe but, in those days, it was customary. Just like in these days it's customary when we don't pay our mortgage for the bank to foreclose on our home. If we don't pay, we can't stay. When we don't pay our car note, it's customary for the finance company to repossess our car. If we don't pay, the car can't stay.

Fearlessly, this widow entreated the assistance of the Prophet because she had first hand knowledge of his ability as a true man of God. Faithfully, she executed his instructions because she trusted in his ability as a true man of God.

As her sons borrowed empty jars from friends and neighbors, she filled them to capacity with the only thing she had to give – the one jar of oil she had to her name. Because of her obedience to the man of God, her little jar of oil was multiplied. Like the woman with the blood disease whose *faith* divinely connected her to Jesus' anointing, this widow's faith divinely connected her to Elisha's anointing.

In the beginning when God said, *"Be fruitful, and multiply"*, He could just as easily have said, *"Be fruitful, and add"* but the product of multiplying two or more quantities together generally results in a much larger number than the aggregate of adding two or more quantities.

Actually, in this case, God used addition and multiplication. When the widow placed her little oil in the Master's plan, He added to it and it multiplied.

People of God, it is not the will of God for us to be in debt. We are encouraged in Romans 13:8 (NIV) to *"let no debt remain outstanding, except the continuing debt to love one another."* Deuteronomy 15:6 says we are lenders not borrowers.

"Those who borrow are slaves of moneylenders."

Proverbs 22:7 CEV

If you've ever been in debt, you know this to be true. The money-hungry money lenders will track you down at home, on your job, in the street and harass you until you pay them every last dime you owe them. Forget the fact that because of the miracle of compound interest, they've already been paid three times over.

God desires for us to be well provided for. Because this widow did what was right with what she had left, after all the jars were filled and the oil ceased, she had *more than enough* money to pay the debt she owed. She had *more than enough* money for her and her two sons to live an abundant life of power, peace and prosperity thereafter.

Let the people of God say…

"GOD IS BIG ON OVERFLOW!"

Let's fast forward to the New Testament where we find the story about an overflow of fish in Luke 5:1-11 (NLT). So many places we could go with this one too but we'll stay focused on the issue at hand – overflow. Jesus, after ministering to the multitudes from Simon Peter's boat, instructed him to take the boat out a little deeper to catch some fish.

> **"'Master,' Simon replied, 'we worked hard all last night and didn't catch a thing. *But if you say so…*'"**

After a long night's work, it was apparent that these fishermen were exhausted from their efforts to get a catch. In spite of their fatigue and frustration, they made the choice to obey the Word of the Lord. So they pushed out into the deep and let their nets down for a catch.

When they raised their nets up out of the water, there was such an overflow of fish that the nets began to break. There was such an overflow of fish that they had to call for their partners in another boat to come help them haul the fish in. There was such an overflow of fish that both boats were filled to capacity and began to sink!

The essence of both stories is about the dynamic duo, trust and obedience.

Let the people of God say…

"GOD IS BIG ON OVERFLOW!"

Yes, God is big on overflow but in order to experience a continual and smooth stream of blessings above and beyond what we could ask, think or imagine – we have got to stay *in God's flow*.

The widow obeyed the Prophet Elisha because she trusted in his ability as a true man of God. She trusted in his ability as a true man of God because she had first hand knowledge about Elisha.

Peter was obedient to Jesus' command because he trusted his first hand knowledge that Jesus' was the Son of the living God.

People of God, it's time to detoxify our systems. We must purge our minds and purify our spirits by spending quality time in an intimate One-on-one relationship with the Spirit of God so that we will not be deluded by distorted doctrine and deceptive data but will discipline ourselves to trust His divine declarations and be obedient to his directions.

It was never God's intention for us to settle and struggle. But because of our lack of knowledge and trust in Him, we refuse to obey Him, have settled for the devil's lies (deceptive data) and as a result struggling has become second nature in our lives.

That is NOT the divine design God had in mind when He created mankind.

It is crucial that we master our minds to the reality that the Ministry of Finance is just as much a Ministry as the New Believers Ministry, the Marriage Ministry, the Singles' Ministry, the Music Ministry, etc.

In fact, just as each of these ministries hold bi-weekly or monthly meetings, I believe churches should implement a Finance Ministry that *teaches* the people of God why and how to become responsible stewards of all that God has entrusted us with.

People are not being taught the truth about why to give nor are they being taught how to give.

Let the people of God say…

"WE NEED TO BE TAUGHT 'WHY' AND 'HOW'".

Dave Ramsey's Financial Peace University (FPU) is a 13-week video-curriculum that teaches believers how to manage money God's way. It is a life-changing program that offers biblical and practical principles on how to achieve your financial goals. FPU is a life-changing program that has helped more than one million families change their family tree forever.

A sine qua non extension to FPU is *Momentum: Building the Kingdom debt free* workshop. This workshop is designed to teach church leaders how to lead their congregation to financial maturity by cultivating a culture of generosity in the church and in the community.

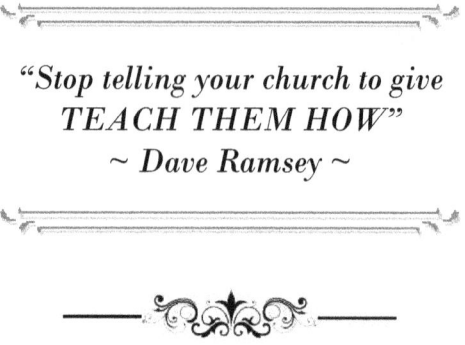

"Stop telling your church to give TEACH THEM HOW"
~ Dave Ramsey ~

The dynamic duo, trust and obedience are like conjoined twins. Although modern science has made it possible to successfully separate conjoined twins, trust and obedience can never be separated successfully without experiencing consequences and repercussions.

We can't do one and not the other. We can't say we trust God and then disobey Him and we can't obey God if we don't trust Him.

Everything the enemy "creates" is a perversion of what God created. Why should this be any different?

The enemy works restlessly and ruthlessly to pervert the "prosperity message" because he knows the inherent power in our cheerful, consistent giving.

Satan knows that the wealth of the sinner is stored up for the righteous and will eventually find its way into our hands (Proverbs 13:22). He knows that in order for us to tap into it, we must do things in God's divine order.

He knows that if we operate effectively and efficiently under our New Covenant, he won't be as firmly positioned to deceive us as he has been in times past but we will be firmly positioned to receive from God.

Our New Covenant with God empowers us to walk worthy in our destiny of dominion and live out God's divine design for our life…in this life.

Our lack of knowledge concerning our New Covenant with God has left us powerless, walking weakly, being dominated and living life by default.

Abraham understood the nature of his covenant with God. The Abrahmic Covenant is an unconditional covenant in which God made promises to Abram that required nothing of Abram (Genesis 12:1-3). Even so, in Genesis 22:2 (NIV), we find God making an unusual request of Abraham…

> **"Then God said, 'Take your son, your only son, Isaac, whom you love, and go to the region of Moriah. Sacrifice him there as a burnt offering on one of the mountains I will tell you about.'"**

Because Abraham had an intimate One-on-one relationship with God and understood the magnitude of his covenant, he trusted God implicitly and obeyed Him immediately…even though this request made no sense to him at all. Abraham's willingness to sacrifice his one and only son, Isaac in response to God's confusing command paved the way for God to sacrifice His one and only Son, Jesus.

Remember, God never requires us to give because He needs what we have, He requires us to give because *we* need what *He* has.

Later in Genesis 22:17, after His encounter with Abraham on Mount Moriah, God declared and decreed…

> **"That in blessing I will bless thee, and in multiplying I will multiply thy seed as the stars of the heaven."**

Not only was Abraham blessed beyond measure that day because of his willingness, obedience and trust, *we* were blessed beyond measure that day. Abraham's willingness, obedience and trust enabled God to give us His Best so we could live a blessed life…now and later.

It IS the will of God that we live in the overflow.

When Abraham sent his servant to find a wife for Isaac in Genesis 24:34-35 (NIV), his servant made this formal announcement…

> **"I am Abraham's servant. The LORD has blessed my master abundantly, and he has become wealthy."**

Our New Covenant is based on *better promises*. Can you imagine that? I CAN! But for our Master to bless us abundantly, we must stay *in His flow* where overflow is inevitable!

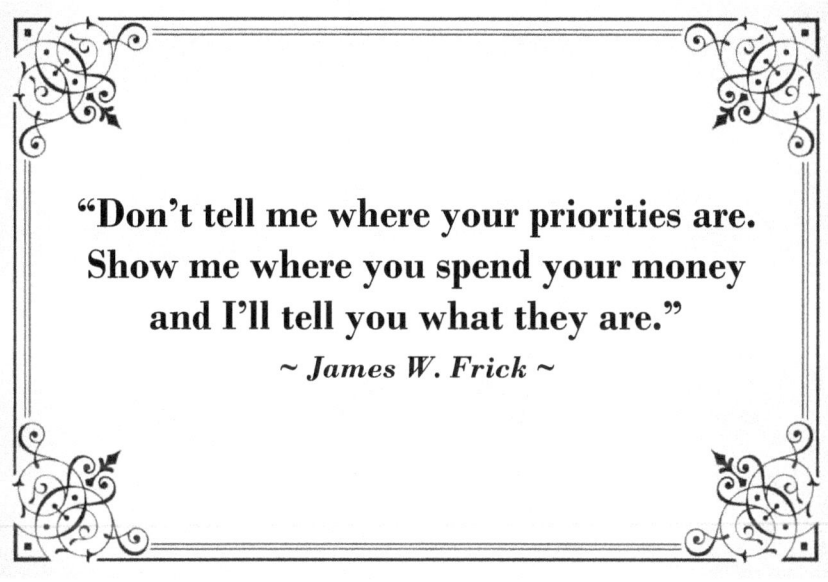

"Don't tell me where your priorities are. Show me where you spend your money and I'll tell you what they are."
~ *James W. Frick* ~

THE MASTER DECISION

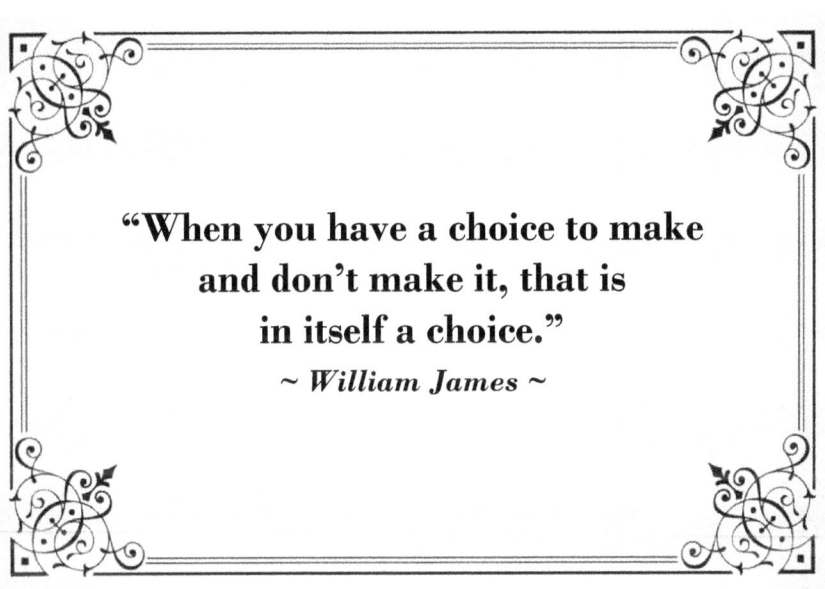

"When you have a choice to make
and don't make it, that is
in itself a choice."
~ *William James* ~

DECIDE TO ABIDE

  This current economy is in dire straits. The expression "in this economy" is the standard prelude or postlude of almost every conversation these days. While it is indeed a sad state of affairs and a true indicator of end time events, the miserable state of this current economy should not have come as a surprise to the people of God who meditate on and have knowledge of the Word of God.

  The miserable state of this current economy is the fulfillment of the law of seedtime and harvest. It is nothing more than the harvest of the seeds of greed that have been sown down through the years.

> **"Be not deceived; God is not mocked: for whatsoever a man soweth, that shall he also reap."**
>
> **Galatians 6:7**

Daily, people are scrambling for solutions and searching for a sense of security, to no avail. This economic earthquake should not have shaken up the children of God the way it has shaken up the children of disobedience.

While the rest of the world frantically scrambles for solutions and searches for security, the children of God should find solace and surety in the reality that God gave us His Best.

Why, then, have we chosen to settle for less?

We've already determined that identity theft has created an identity crisis that has inhibited the ability of some believers to believe that God's promises *already* belong to us and therefore impeded their ability to receive the promises of God but this identity crisis has also infused even more fear into this atmosphere of fear.

Fear is rampant. The fear factor is probably higher than it's ever been…especially during this current economic earthquake. Everywhere we turn fear is blatantly glaring at us in the face.

Fear of terrorism, fear of layoffs, fear of financial lack, fear of foreclosure, fear of bad credit, fear of fluctuating gas prices, fear of escalating food prices, fear of strange weather patterns, fear of natural disasters, fear of life-threatening sicknesses and fear of death has gripped and paralyzed the minds of nonbelievers and believers alike.

False **E**vidence **A**ppears **R**eal when we allow fear to overrule our evidence of things not seen – faith.

Our native tongue, before we get born-again, is laden with fear and our native mind is filled with thoughts driven by fear because the world we live in is saturated with fear.

Fear-based thinking results in fear-based speaking. If our mind is saturated with fearful thoughts, we will speak fearful words.

Faith-based thinking results in faith-based speaking. If our mind is saturated with powerful thoughts, our mouth will speak powerful words.

Fear-based thinking and speaking magnifies the so-called giants in our life.

Remember the ten spies who were sent to scout out the Promised Land? They allowed what they *saw* – the deliberate distractions in the Promised Land – to dictate what they *thought* and ultimately, what they thought dictated what they *said*...

> **"And there we saw giants...and we were in our own sight as grasshoppers, and so we were in their sight."**
> **Numbers 13:33**

The fear of what they saw saturated their minds with fearful thoughts that attracted more fearful thoughts.

Not only did they see themselves as grasshoppers, they thought the giants saw them as grasshoppers too. Now, how did they know what the giants were thinking?

Instead of walking in their destiny of dominion – which was to possess the land of Promise God had *already* given them, they began to analyze the deliberate distractions, which paralyzed their faith, severed their divine connection with God and cost them their inheritance.

Fear-based thinking and speaking is the life-support these so-called giants thrive on to survive in our lives.

If we allow fear to interfere with our focus on our faith, like the ten spies, the giants will intimidate us and infiltrate our mind with fear. As we begin to analyze these deliberate distractions, it will paralyze our faith, sever our divine connection with God and cost us our inheritance.

That's why it's imperative that we master our mind to believe that God's Word is absolutely true. We must not allow our minds to wander away from God's promises or wonder if God's promises are real for us in this life.

Once we master our mind to believe God implicitly, we must master our mouth to speak God's Word immediately to *every* giant that steps foot in our domain. We must use our divine ammunition to eliminate the disturbing dialect of death and defeat these despicable giants that threaten our quality of life.

We cannot allow what these so-called giants present to us to take precedence over what God has *already* promised us.

> *We must DECIDE TO ABIDE by God's Word.*

Jesus promises us in John 15:7 – that if we abide in Him (dwell with Him, remain in Him and stay connected to Him) and allow His words to abide in us (dwell with us, remain in us and stay connected to us) that we can be sure that whatever we ask our Father would be done for us.

Let the people of God say…

"Divine Connection Guarantees Divine Intervention."

Fear is the biggest giant that needs to be demolished in our life.

"For God has not given us a spirit of fear and timidity, but of power, love, and self-discipline."

2 Timothy 1:7 NLT

God has given us a divine arsenal of lethal weapons – power over ALL the power of the enemy (Luke 10:19), His love that's been poured in our hearts by the Holy Spirit (Romans 5:5) and the sound mind of Christ (1 Corinthians 2:16) – that activates the spirit of faith that eradicates the spirit of fear.

Let the people of God say…

"Fear is NOT from God."

The spirit of fear that has encased this earth was initiated by the father of lies, not the Father of lights. He works relentlessly and resolutely to keep this atmosphere saturated with fear because he knows that his spirit of fear makes it impossible for us to please God. He knows that his spirit of fear has severe ramifications on our spirit of faith. He knows that his spirit of fear is adverse to our spirit of faith.

Faith liberates...fear suffocates
Faith mobilizes...fear paralyzes
Faith participates...fear hesitates
Faith concentrates...fear deviates
Faith receives...fear deceives

Faith and fear cannot coexist. They're like oil and water; they don't mix. As darkness cannot exist in the presence of light, fear cannot exist in the presence of faith.

Faith brings God on the scene.
Fear brings Satan on the scene.

Faith is responsible for our ability to release the promises of God in our life. Fear is responsible for our inability to receive the promises of God in our life.

The enemy uses the false evidence we see with our natural eyes to influence what we think and what we say. That's why God commands us to *"walk by faith, not by sight"* (2 Corinthians 5:7).

If we are living in fear, we are not living or walking by faith as is our calling. There is no in-between; no gray area. It's all or nothing at all.

The enemy knows that fear is the only thing that can limit God's unlimited power in the life of every believer because it severs our divine connection to God. I say the only thing because all the "other" things – disbelief and disobedience – are triggered by fear.

Fear hinders us from being obedient to God and believing God and disobedience and disbelief hinder us from being blessed by God.

I don't know about you but every time a life-changing event is about to occur in my life...the spirit of fear will show up dressed to the nines. As I was writing this book, the spirit of fear emerged from the deepest pits of hell presenting all kinds of mental monstrosities devised to paralyze me from completing my assignment.

But I'm here to tell you, *God is an awesome God*. We can go to Him anytime about anything. He is a very present help in time of trouble. I sought the Lord and He delivered me from all my fears.

He delivered me from the spirit of procrastination and self-sabotage. He delivered me from my fear of failure *and* success. He delivered me from my fear of rejection *and* acceptance. You see, that's how fear works; it plays both ends of the stick against the middle.

Fear will do whatever it takes to keep us from fulfilling our destiny and receiving our inheritance.

Oh but I PRAISE GOD that the spirit of faith swelled up BIG in my Inside Man and swallowed up that spirit of fear. I PRAISE GOD that that same spirit of faith boldly and confidently *believes and speaks* that this anointed, self-published book will premiere on the NY Times Best Seller list and supernaturally sell one million copies within one year!

> **"For with God *nothing is ever impossible* and not one word from God shall be without power or *impossible of fulfillment.*"**
> **Luke 1:37 AMP**

But more importantly than the sales of this book, are the one million souls that will be won into the Kingdom of God as a result of reading this book.

Even if only one person repents and turns or returns to God, there will be *"more joy in heaven than over ninety-nine others who are righteous and haven't strayed away"* (Luke 15:7 NLT)!

Let the people of God say...

TO GOD BE THE GLORY!

God's directive for His people to live/walk by faith is not contingent on the circumstances – what the situation looks like, how we feel about the situation or what we heard about the situation. When we allow these deliberate distractions to deceive us and govern our actions, the enemy becomes our puppeteer and you'd better believe that he won't hesitate to manipulate every step we take and every move we make every change he gets.

While on this earth, we know that Jesus lived and walked by faith because He *decided to abide* by His Father's Word. He didn't allow deliberate distractions to deceive Him or deter Him from fulfilling His destiny of dominion. He came to do what God sent Him to do (John 6:38) and say what God sent Him to say (John 12:49). He was able to live a faith-filled life because He maintained a secure divine connection with His Father...and that pleased His Father.

> **"...behold a voice out of the cloud, which said, This is my beloved Son, *in whom I am well pleased.*"**
>
> **Matthew 17:5**

God was only able to operate effectively and efficiently in Jesus' life because Jesus created and operated in an atmosphere of faith.

Likewise, God is only able to operate effectively and efficiently in our lives when we create and operate in an atmosphere of faith.

Whenever a life-changing event was about to occur in the Word, the first command given was *"fear not"* or *"be not afraid"* because God absolutely cannot and will not operate in an atmosphere of fear.

Indulge me for a moment as I share two significant life-changing events that speak to God's power operating effectively and efficiently in a faith-filled atmosphere.

The first, one of my favorites, is the story of Jairus, the father who exercised extreme faith in an extremely fearful situation. Jairus, a highly respected Jewish leader of the synagogue, had a little girl who was very ill to the point of death. I'm sure every parent can appreciate the full range of emotions Jairus was experiencing and I'm certain that every parent will agree that during such a critical time, remaining at your child's side would be your number one priority.

Jairus probably wanted to stay and would have stayed by his daughter's side but the thought of losing her without at least trying to get her some help was too much for him to bear. Jairus probably could have stayed by his daughters' side, waiting fearfully for the inevitable, but he decided to press past the haze of fear that attempted to overwhelm him long enough to take a journey of faith that would forever change his life, his wife's life, his daughter's life and our life.

Yes, Jairus could have sent a representative to approach Jesus and make this appeal of healing on his behalf but he was not going to risk delegating this crucial task to one of his servants to carry out. This was *his* daughter's life that hung in the balance and it was *his* responsibility to make this journey.

This was a personal problem that required his personal attention because he knew she needed a personal touch from the Master.

Let the people of God say...

"ONE TOUCH CHANGES EVERYTHING."

As this reputable Jewish leader bustled his way through the massive crowd that besieged Jesus, his position of prominence did not take precedence in his mind because he was too preoccupied with the current condition of his precious princess – his only baby girl.

He was oblivious to what others might think or say about his act of humility as he fell at Jesus' feet, earnestly pleading...

> **"My little daughter is dying. Please come and put your hands on her so that she will be healed and live."**
>
> Mark 5:23 NLT

Jairus didn't mince words. He clearly communicated his problem – *my little daughter is dying*; his petition – *please come and put your hands on her*; and his presumption – *so that she will be healed and live*.

It doesn't appear that much transpired between Jairus' request and Jesus' resolve because in the very next verse we find that…

"Jesus went with him."

With no questions asked and no comments made, Jesus went with him. What was it that made Jesus stop what He was doing or postpone what He was about to do and just go with Jairus?

Jesus recognized the spirit of faith in Jairus.

Jairus *believed* that one touch from the Master would change the outcome of his situation and he *spoke* accordingly. His earnest plea for divine intervention was direct and decisive just as his corresponding action – his decision to make this journey of faith – was definite and deliberate.

Let the people of God say…

"The Spirit of Faith Believes and Speaks."

Jesus will always commit Himself to us when we commission Him in faith.

While en route to Jairus' house, Jesus experiences another close encounter with the spirit of faith that seizes His attention…the woman with the "issue of blood".

In those days, having an issue of blood was a serious issue to have. In the entire fifteenth chapter of the book of Leviticus, the Lord speaks extensively about bodily discharges and details stipulations and consequences concerning this unsanitary condition.

Can you imagine the drama this issue of blood caused this woman? She was a social outcast because of her unsanitary condition.

Can you imagine her frustration after twelve long years of doctor visits being poked and prodded, with still no clue about what could be done about her condition?

I'm certain the speculation about her situation became increasingly spectacular as the years went by. *"What's the matter with Sister Sue? Is she still bleeding? Well you know what I heard…"*

In the minds of her family and friends, surely she must have committed some terrible sin that caused this horrible disease to plague her. (Remember Job's family and friends?)

Can you imagine how vulnerable she felt? This debilitating disease was no walk in the park.

Ladies, keeping it real, how weak do we feel after *one week* of bleeding?

Twelve long years of profuse bleeding no doubt weakened her physically and drained her mentally. Emotionally, she had to be exhausted being estranged from her family and friends and spiritually, after hearing all the *"Blah, blah, blah"* she too probably wondered what in the world was going on? What she could have possibly done so wrong to deserve this "curse"?

This woman was at the end of her rope; desperate to find a solution to her situation. After twelve years of hearing bleak diagnoses, listening to grim prognoses and ingesting all types of medications to retard the bleeding, to no avail, she had to be experiencing fear on so many levels.

And then…she heard about Jesus. And when she heard about Jesus, the Word says, she pressed in.

The Master Decision

It is no coincidence that the placement of Mark's account of this story in the fifth chapter immediately follows his account of Jesus' parable of the Sower in the fourth chapter. This woman's story is the personification of the fourth heart in that parable that *received* the seed sown.

> **"But the seed planted in the good earth represents those who hear the Word, embrace it, and produce a harvest beyond their wildest dreams."**
>
> **Mark 4:20 MSG**

Even though this woman *"was no better but instead grew worse"* (Mark 5:26 AMP), when the seed that Jesus was a Healer was *planted*, she *embraced* it eagerly and enthusiastically and because she acted on it, she *produced* an extraordinary harvest of healing.

The *Amplified Bible* says…

> **"For she kept saying, If I only touch His garments, I shall be restored to health."**
>
> **Mark 5:28**

This woman meditated on the word she heard day and night. The original Hebrew word translated *"meditate"* in Joshua 1:8 means *"to moan, utter, mutter, muse, imagine"*.

I can imagine this woman muttering – *"I shall be restored"* – under her breath over and over. As she uttered these words, I imagine that she imagined herself healed.

Slowly but persistently, she pressed through this great assembly of people as she headed toward Jesus. You know, she was taking a great risk imposing herself and her unsanitary condition on this crowd. Jesus was always surrounded by a multitude of people. So just think about how many people she came in contact with as she made her way to Him. And remember, everything and everybody she came in contact was deemed ceremonially unclean.

The thought probably never even crossed her mind. Even if it did, her heart was fixed and her mind was made up. She *believed* what she had heard about Jesus and she would not be deterred.

How do we know she believed?

She kept saying … *"I shall be restored"* not *"I might be restored"*, *"I shall be restored"*. (Faith comes by hearing.)

Something on the inside was working on the outside. She had a press in her spirit that pressed past her fear, her pain and her poverty.

I imagine that the closer she got to Jesus, the thicker the crowd was and the more difficult it was for her to maneuver through the crowd. This thickness could have easily dissuaded her but the press in her spirit persuaded her to press in and press on.

She pressed past the embarrassment. She pressed past her discomfort. She pressed past the condemnation.

She had come this far by faith and she was determined to get what she came for. She wasn't about to allow what was going on around her to influence what was going on inside her.

She pressed past all the mess and pressed toward her destination: transformation!

The Word says she came up behind Jesus and touched the hem of His garment. I can see her scooching down and reaching in, stretching her arms and wiggling her fingers, her face pressed into the dirt (you know how we do when we're reaching for something under the bed that's out of our reach) until…she touched His hem; until…she touched Him.

*Instantly t*he bleeding stopped and she was changed.

Let the people of God say…

"One Touch Changes Everything."

This woman *believed* what she heard, she *said* what she believed and she *received* what she believed. That press in her spirit extinguished her fear and executed her faith in Jesus' ability to heal her ailment.

Now when Jesus realized what had happened, He asked…

"Who touched me?"

What? Who touched You? Seriously Jesus?

Why would Jesus ask such a question as He stood deep in the midst of a multitude of people who were pushing and pulling, tugging and shoving Him – all trying to get a piece of Him?

Why? Because *this* touch was different. *This* touch was special. *This* touch was unlike any other touch He had felt that day. *This* touch was fueled with faith.

Just as this woman's declaration for divine intervention was direct and decisive, her corresponding actions – her decision to make this journey of faith and her touch of faith – were definite and deliberate.

"Someone deliberately touched me, for I felt healing power go out from me."

Clearly there were others in the crowd touching Jesus *hoping* to be healed (and Jesus healed them all) but this woman touched Jesus *expecting* to be healed.

> *Divine Intervention responds*
> *to Divine Expectation.*

The magnetism of her touch of faith forced healing power to liberally flow out of Jesus.

Jesus was probably thinking…*"Somebody finally got it! Somebody finally understands the power of faith to change everything!"*

As she came forward to tell Jesus her story, Jesus said…

"Daughter, *thy faith hath made thee whole*; go in peace, and be whole of thy plague."
Mark 5:34

There is significance to Jesus' choice of words in this passage of scripture.

Had this woman allowed her faith to succumb to fear, she would not have received her healing. Not because Jesus' anointing to heal was altered – Jesus' anointing to heal is constant – but because her fear would have kept her from *connecting* to Jesus' healing anointing. Instead, *her faith* divinely connected her to Jesus' healing anointing and she was made whole.

One definition of the word "wholeness" is *"not broken, damaged, or impaired, intact"*. Because of her faith, whatever was broken or damaged or impaired in her life was now intact. Jesus bid her to *"go in peace"* because a life of wholeness produces a life of peace.

Meanwhile, Jairus stood quietly next to Jesus watching this transpire. Initially, my thought was surely his mind had to be spinning. Time was of the essence and here he was at a standstill listening to this woman go on and on about her life story. This interruption just might cost his daughter her life.

But there is no indication anywhere in the Word that Jairus' demeanor changed at all.

The Spirit reminded me that the reason Jairus was able to maintain his composure through this whole ordeal was because his earnest plea for divine intervention was direct and decisive. He had already said what he needed to say and because he *believed* what he said, there was no need for him to say anything else.

* P A U S E   &   P O N D E R *

Just as they were about to resume their journey, the enemy came in like a flood trying to shift the atmosphere from faith to fear. Jairus was approached by his servants bearing news that should have pushed him over the edge – news of the demise of his sweet little girl.

The Master Decision

Overhearing and ignoring this evil report, Jesus intervened and immediately spoke words of confirmation and comfort before Jairus could retract his confession...

> **"Be not afraid, only believe."**
> **Mark 5:36**

...and they continued on their way. When they finally arrived at Jairus' house, once again Jesus had to dismiss the spirit of fear so He could create an atmosphere that was conducive for Him to operate effectively and efficiently.

> **"Holding her hand, he said to her, 'Talitha koum,' which means 'Little girl, get up!' And the girl, who was twelve years old, immediately stood up and walked around! They were overwhelmed and totally amazed."**
> **Mark 5:41-42 NLT**

What does any of this have to do with you?

Well, the very moment you *decide to abide* by God's Word to renew your thinking, refresh your speaking and reform your spending all hell *will* break loose all around you – in your marriage, in your family, on your job, in your church.

The moment you *decide to abide* by God's Word, the more imposing the issues will seem, the more irritating the interruptions will become and the more intense the infirmities will be – trying to shake you to your core. I'm telling you what I know. My humble advice to you is this...

> *You shouldn't always believe what you see;*
> *But you should always see what you believe.*

Remember, what we say has the power to change what we see. Jairus and the woman with the issue of blood said what they believed and changed what he saw.

Had Jairus looked at his dismal situation and believed what he saw with his natural eyes, his daughter would have died. Instead, he chose to see *and* say what he believed – that his daughter would live if she received one touch from the Master.

Had the woman with the issue of blood looked at her grim plight and believed what she saw with her natural eyes, she would have been stuck with her "issue" for the rest of her life. Instead, she chose to see *and* say what she believed – that her health would be restored with just one touch from the Master.

No matter how dismal and grim our situation is, we must choose to see *and* say what we believe – that we can live a new life of power, peace and prosperity with just one touch from the Master.

Let the people of God say…

"ONE TOUCH CHANGES EVERYTHING."

The spirit of fear that will approach you during this time will be supercharged to the 10th power. The devil is always up on his game and you can trust and believe that he is going to turn up the heat. He never relinquishes anyone or anything without a fight.

Well, people of God, it's time for us to step up on our game and get ready to fight back with the divine arsenal of lethal weapons God has given us to fight this good fight of faith because you do realize that our faith is what the enemy is ultimately after.

> *It's time we stop letting the devil devour OUR power!*

It's time for us to master our mind to believe that God gave us His Best and because His Best did the rest, we've got the power!

It's time to master our mouth to speak about the goodness of Jesus, to worship Him for Who He is and praise Him what He's done!

Recently, the Spirit spoke to me and said *"My people can't worship Me for Who I Am in spirit and in truth because the truth is they don't know Who I Am in their spirit. They can't offer a sacrifice of praise for what I've done because they don't fully grasp the magnitude of sacrifice I made."*

When this spirit of fear comes, we can either decide to sit by the wayside and be capsized or we can *decide to abide* by God's Word.

We can either allow fear to interfere with our faith or we can use our faith to domineer fear!

We can either allow our circumstances to change our confession or we can use our confession to change our circumstances.

When this spirit of fear comes, we must execute the spirit of faith and extinguish the spirit of fear.

The spirit of faith is a commanding spirit. It doesn't deviate, speculate or fluctuate. It articulates and mandates and fixates on the hope it affirms because the spirit of faith knows God has *already* kept His promise.

While on this journey, we will encounter those who will try to discourage us and ridicule us and talk all manner of evil against us falsely because we have *decided to abide* by God's Word. As the evidence of our transformation increases, their speculation will become increasingly spectacular. *"Who does she think she is? I remember her when…"*

We must not allow what people say to move our emotions because our emotions move our lips. We must decide to only be moved by *what we believe.*

Back-up is just one prayer away. Twenty-four hours a day, 7 days a week, we can run to the Throne (not the phone) to make an earnest plea for divine intervention that is direct and decisive and to receive that extra strength we need to take action that is definite and deliberate.

Destination: Transformation

If you have ever been involved in a renovation, you know that the first step in the process of renovation is demolition. Old stuff has to be torn down before new stuff can be built up. Old stuff needs to be gutted out before new stuff can be loaded in.

During this renovation, the worksite being renovated may not be a pretty sight with its broken walls, shattered windows and damaged floors.

As stressful as this phase may be, we endure it because our focus is on the end result – not on what things look like at the moment. We realize that there is a process involved to make the vision on the blueprint visible.

Destination: Transformation is "renovation" for the born-again believer. Old stuff must be torn down before new stuff can be built up. Old stuff needs to be gutted out before new stuff can be loaded in.

> **"And no one puts new wine into old wineskins. For the new wine would burst the wineskins, spilling the wine and ruining the skins. New wine must be stored in new wineskins."**
> **Luke 5:37-38 NLT**

So it's out with the old and in with the new – out with the world's finite way of thinking and in with the Word's infinite way of thinking. It's out with the world's powerless way of speaking and in with the Word's powerful way of speaking.

David, a man after God's own heart, understood the importance of the mind-mouth connection...

> **"Let the words of my mouth, and the meditation of my heart, be acceptable in thy sight, O LORD, my strength, and my redeemer."**
>
> **Psalm 19:14**

During this renovation, what we see may not always be pretty – broken hearts, shattered dreams and damaged relationships. As challenging as the process may be, we must master our mind to endure this transition to transformation. We must realize that this process is necessary to make the vision in the blueprint of our mind visible in our life.

During this renovation, we must stay divinely connected to God regarding our thinking…

> **"Search me, O God, and know my heart; test me and know my anxious thoughts. Point out anything in me that offends you, and lead me along the path of everlasting life."**
>
> **Psalm 139:23-24 NLT**

…and our speaking…

> **"Set a guard over my mouth, O LORD; keep watch over the door of my lips."**
>
> **Psalm 141:3 NIV**

During this renovation, we must master our mind to focus on the end result and master our mouth to speak the end result… VICTORY *in Christ*.

A mastered mind doesn't focus on what things look like at the moment; a mastered mind focuses on what things will look like in a moment…God's moment not ours.

A mastered mind understands that the promises of God are inherited through faith and patience.

A mastered mind can wait faithfully and patiently because the belief of a mastered mind extends beyond just knowing that God can or knowing that God will; a mastered mind knows that *God already has.*

Romans 4:17 (AMP) tells us that God speaks of nonexistent things – things He has prophesied and promised – as if they already exist...because in God's mind, they already exist.

> *Everything God said...God saw.*

God says in Isaiah 55:11 that when He sends out His Word, it will not return without producing what it's been sent to produce, without accomplishing what it's been sent to accomplish, without prospering in what it's been sent to prosper in.

In the same vein, every Word of promise God has sent out to us is *already* ours. But it's up to us to take possession of these promises by faith. It's up to us to master our mind to *believe* that these promises have *already* been accomplished in our life and to live the prosperous life that these promises produce.

It's up to us to master our mouth to continually *speak* God's promises over our life until they manifest in our life.

If we don't claim by faith – *believing and speaking* – what God has *already* decreed belongs to us...shame on us.

Let the people of God say...

"THE SPIRIT OF FAITH BELIEVES AND SPEAKS."

However, if during this renovation, we stay focused on the deliberate distractions that the enemy will strategically place in our lives to deceive us and divert our attention from what's *already* ours and continue to *speak* death and curses over our life, we will continue to *see* death and curses in our life.

Destination: Transformation begins with a quality decision. A quality decision is premeditated and purposeful. A quality decision stays on course with laser-beam focus.

Most believers have a "flashlight mentality". Flashlights release light in many directions, and the light is very weak and diffuse. Most believers have been searching in many different directions for all the right answers...in all the wrong places. That's how the enemy keeps us distracted and deceived.

Laser-beams are very directional with an *extremely* tight beam focus that is strong and concentrated. When a laser beam is concentrated in an extremely tight focus and pulsed at the highest frequency, it is strong enough to cut through steel.

If we are to successfully thwart the deliberate distractions and demonic deceptions of the enemy, we must exchange our flashlight mentality for a laser-beam focused mindset that is very directional with an *extremely* tight beam focus that is strong and concentrated on the Word.

The quality decision we make is to believe that God is Who He says He is and that He has *already* done what He said He did.

On that "promise", we *decide to abide* by His Word. We re-direct our focus from destroying and sabotaging to developing and strengthening our recreated newborn spirit – our Inside Man.

As spirit beings, what's goes on inside of us is far more important than what's going on outside because what's goes on inside of us has the ability to change what's going on outside.

To a certain extent, external elements affect us internally but to a greater extent our internal elements have far more of an affect on our external reality. That's why we must firmly commit to nourishing our spirits with the proper nutrients it needs to grow in grace, to glow as candles shining brightly in the darkness and to produce overflow in every area of our lives.

We have absolute and total control over what registers on our Inside Man. Up until now, we have allowed our spirits to digest data that has been detrimental, not instrumental, to our spiritual health and development.

The recent results of Nielsen's "Three Screen Report" showed that the average American watches approximately 153 hours of TV every month at home, a 1.2% increase from last year.

That means that 20% of our day is spent watching a gamut of television programs that add absolutely no real value to our life.

Remember, according to the Bureau of Labor Statistics "American Time Use Survey" conducted in 2009, *"watching TV was the leisure activity that occupied the most time."*

Factor in the remaining leisure activities most people engage in during the course of a twenty-hour day – work, school, household chores, caretaking – and you will find that the average American spends most of their time focused on "outside" activities – activities designed by the enemy to keep us BUSY (**B**urdened **U**nder **S**atan's **Y**oke) doing what appears to be important so we don't have enough time (or energy) to do what's *really* important. And he's had great success.

> *America the beautiful has become America the busy!*

"Multi-tasking" is now the norm in our society and believers are going right with the flow – doing what needs to be done to make sure the bills are paid so we can live "comfortably" in nice homes (with upside-down mortgages) and drive nice cars (with exorbitant monthly payments).

All because looking from the outside in, we need to appear to be keeping up with the Joneses. Newsflash, the "Joneses" are trying to keep up with the Joneses. The Joneses are struggling to keep up with their monthly mortgage payments to prevent foreclosure. The Joneses have put their CLS550 Coupe and 760i Sedan for sale on eBay to pay up those delinquent mortgage payments and credit card bills.

In the grand scheme of things, what's *really* more important – what man sees or what God sees? What man says or what God says?

> **"Man looks at the outward appearance, but the LORD looks at the heart."**
> 1 Samuel 16:7 NIV

Meanwhile, our Inside Man – the man with the plan, the man who can change our external reality – is impaired, in pain, and in turmoil.

This vicious system of "busyness" has been artfully sculpted by the enemy to keep us deliberately distracted from and deceived about what's *really* important.

What's *really* important is spending quality time *with* the Word *in* the Word. Only He can repair our brokenness, remove the pain, renew our messed up minds and replace it all with His power and His peace.

The Pareto principle or the "80/20 rule" as it is more commonly known, states that, for many events, roughly 80% of the effects come from 20% of the causes.

The common rule of thumb in business is 80% of the revenue is generated by 20% of the clients; in industry, 80% of the work is produced by 20% of the employees.

If we were to apply this rule in life, we would realize that 80% of the drama we experience is produced by 20% of the enemy's deliberate distractions.

Let's slightly modify this 80/20 rule to a 90/10 rule: 90% of life's drama would drastically decrease if each day we gave God 10% of the 1,440 minutes He's given us.

If we spent 30 minutes conversing with Him (15 minutes first thing in the morning when we rise and 15 minutes last thing in the evening before we close our eyes), 60 minutes reading and meditating on His Word, 30 minutes confessing His Word over our life and 24 minutes praising Him for His Word, the enemy's distractions would not distract us so often and his deceptions would not deceive us so easily.

During this renovation, it is *our* responsibility to protect, not neglect, the incorruptible seed that has been sown in our spirit to inspire new life *in Christ* by spending quality time immersed in God's Word.

As we first feed on the sincere milk of God's Word and then feast on the strong meat of God's Word, the seed will germinate in our spirit and at the appointed time, the Word will become flesh and dwell among us.

Let me ask you this: What is the likelihood that you can go to an ATM machine and make a withdrawal if you have no funds in your bank account?

It's a simple analogy but the reality is many believers are trying to make "withdrawals" from Heaven's repository without having made any "deposits" in their earthly depository.

They won't make the time to consistently deposit God's Word in their hearts but they fully expect to have the promises of God deposited into their life.

Let the people of God say…

"No Deposit…No Return!"

That's not how the law of seedtime and harvest works. Nothing is reaped until something is sown. We can't expect to reap the benefits of the Word until we sow the basics of the Word in our spirit.

Our "flashlight mentality" has us spending big money and devoting our valuable time reading books, listening to CDs, watching DVDs and attending seminars offered by "experts" who have taken spiritual laws and biblical principles instituted by the Master of the Universe – renamed them, reworded them, removed "God" from the equation – and applied them to their life to achieve unprecedented success.

Spellbound, we sit on the sidelines glamorizing and fantasizing about their achievements when what we should be doing is meditating on God's principles so we can appropriate God's promises into our life.

"Non-believers" have gained a greater appreciation for the mind-mouth connection than most believers and have capitalized on it.

Believers have gained a greater respect for what the world has to say about how to achieve "the secret" than what the Word has to say.

The sad reality is believers spend more money financing the kingdom of darkness than they spend financing Kingdom business.

Believers spend more money trying to find out "how to" live a more fulfilling life and make more money listening to experts that literally make more money *teaching us* how to make more money.

In his Preface Psalm, David tells us...

> **"BLESSED (HAPPY, fortunate, prosperous, and enviable) is the man who walks and lives not in the counsel of the ungodly [following their advice, their plans and purposes]."**
> **Psalm 1:1AMP**

The "Law of Affirmation", which affirms Jesus' declaration in Mark 11:23, proclaims that whatever goals we repeat repeatedly in a positive tone with a personal touch in the present tense will be accepted by our subconscious as commands to be executed in our life.

As we affirm – declare or confess solemnly and formally as true – what God says about us in His Word, we will begin seeing what God says we should see and having what God says we should have.

The "Law of Attraction" proclaims that we attract into our life whatever we think about most.

Joshua 1:8 is the original Law of Attraction. As we meditate – intently reflect on and engage in thought about God's Word – we attract the wisdom of God.

> **"Wisdom is the principal thing."**
> **Proverbs 4:7**

Spoken like a true King who when asked by God – *"ask for anything you want, and I will give it to you"*, asked for wisdom and knowledge (1 Chronicles 1:10).

The wisdom of God may be foolishness to man, but know that the *"foolish plan of God is wiser than the wisest of human plans, and God's weakness is stronger than the greatest of human strength"* (1 Corinthians 1:25 NLT).

The wisdom of man, which is foolishness to God, is largely responsible for the creation of this chaotic culture that has left so many desperate and in despair. Man's artificial intelligence has left non-believers and believers living crisis-filled lives.

During this renovation, our first priority is to re-prioritize. We must stop the compromise and realize that it would be wise for us to seek *first* God's will and His way of doing and being right in all we do and all we say and let Him lead the way.

Know this…ALL roads will eventually lead back to God.

> "…As I live, saith the Lord, *every knee* shall bow to me, and *every tongue* shall confess to God."
>
> Romans 14:11

This book you now hold in your hands contains a practical three-step course of action that *can absolutely* change what happens **NEXT** in your life. Whether or not this three-step course of action *will* change what happens next in your life is totally dependent on *your* personal course of action.

The Choice Is Yours!

Will you continue living in crisis or start living in Christ?

Will you continue living life by default or start living life by design?

Will you master your mind, your mouth and your money or will you let your mind, your mouth and your money master you?

Will you act on what you've heard and now know or will you continue to act like you haven't heard and don't know.

Whatever you do, have the courage to
Make a Choice!

DIVINE POWER TOOL BOX

Fourteen years ago, my best friend, Wanda, introduced me to an awesome book that changed the course of my life forever. That book was Charles Capps' *The Tongue – A Creative Force*.

After reading this book, I got excited about speaking God's Word over my life to change my world. I got immersed in the Word, and began reading books, listening to teaching tapes/CDs and watching DVDs authored by anointed ministers of the gospel that literally transformed my life.

Although there is no substitute for the Word, these writings and teachings supplement the Word by expounding on specific topics and scriptures and offering life application strategies that make the words in the Word jump off the paper and become real in our life.

The list of books I've compiled, authored by some of these same men and women of God, will augment what you have read here and foster your journey to being transformed to be all that God created you to be and to do all God created you to do.

I guarantee you that as you read these books, you will be further enlightened and empowered to walk this Christian walk with audacity and authority, to live out God's divine design of an abundant life of power, peace and prosperity…in this earth and primed and positioned to live life eternal.

I pray that you've been blessed after reading my book…

From Overdraft to Overflow:
3 Steps to Possession in a Recession

…and that you will be a blessing and spread the Word!

MASTER YOUR MIND
For as he thinks in his heart, so is he.
Proverbs 23:7 AMP

1. **BELIEVING GOD**
   by Beth Moore

   What does it mean to believe God? Abraham and Moses believed God. This planted in them a seed of faith that grew into towering oaks of steadfast trust and belief. Beth Moore brings these characters to life in a way that will spring forth in you a fresh explosion of faith!

2. **IDENTIFIED WITH CHRIST**
   A Complete Cycle from Defeat to Victory
   by Frederick K.C. Price

   Discover how to live the reality of this image in your life, and to not only see yourself identified with Jesus in every area of living, but to make sure that your enemy sees you that way, as well.

3. **THE BATTLEFIELD OF THE MIND**
   Winning the Battle in Your Mind
   by Joyce Meyer

   Worry. Confusion. Anger. Depression. If any of these are a constant companion in your life, there's a battle going on in your mind. You're not alone, though, and the war isn't lost! God wants to fight this for you and this book will teach you how to let Him.

4. **THE BELIEVERS AUTHORITY**
   by Kenneth E. Hagin

   This book clears up many of the misconceptions that exist regarding spiritual authority and will help you discover the authority that rightfully belongs to every believer in Christ.

5. **THE POWER OF IDENTIFICATION IN CHRIST**
   by Mark Hankins

   As a new creature in Christ you have everything you need inside of you to succeed in life! When you see what God has done for you in Christ, the reality of redemption will swallow up your old identity. You've got to overcome your natural identity with your Supernatural Identity! It's in you because you're In Christ!

6. **THOUGHTS: THE BATTLE BETWEEN YOUR EARS**
   by Jerry Savelle

   The most challenging battles you will ever face are the ones between your ears. Dr. Savelle gets to the heart of the matter...the matter of the mind. He candidly shares the consequences of wrong thinking and reveals step-by-step how to win this battle in your thought life.

7. **TRANSFORM YOUR THINKING, TRANSFORM YOUR LIFE**
   Radically Change Your Thoughts, Your World, Your Destiny
   by Bill Winston

   Victory begins with your thought life. Allow God to have His way with your thinking and see the Glory of God manifest in your life. If you are not satisfied with where you are today, try something different. Renew your mind and change positions so that you can look at that situation in a different light.

MASTER YOUR MOUTH

A wise man's heart guides his mouth.
Proverbs 16:23 NIV

1. **FAITH AND CONFESSION**
   How to Activate the Power of God in Your Life
   by Charles Capps

   God's principles of faith and confession unlock the supernatural to work for you! His spiritual, physical and financial provision is available to every believer, but you must understand the methods God has set in motion for your success. Learn how to release God's goodness in your own life. Confessing what God said in His Word out of a heart full of faith will bring God's supernatural intervention. The balance of faith and confession working together is essential for living the abundant life that God has promised.

2. **ME AND MY BIG MOUTH**
   Your Answer is Right Under Your Nose
   by Joyce Meyer

   Is your mouth busy telling all your troubles? Joyce emphasizes that speaking the Word of God, coupled with living in complete obedience to the Word, ignites the full power of God flowing in every area of your life!

3. **SCRIPTURE CONFESSIONS COLLECTION**
   Life Changing Words of Faith for Everyday
   by Keith & Megan Provance

   Whether at work, home, or on the go, you will find powerful, personalized declarations of faith based on the Scriptures that will strengthen you to overcome every challenge. This unique collection of personalized Scripture Confession books includes Victorious Living, Spiritual Growth, Healing, Finances, and Parenting.

4. **THE LAW OF CONFESSION**
   Revolutionize Your Life and Rewrite Your Future with the Power of Words
   by Bill Winston

   Just like natural laws, there are spiritual laws with cause and effect. God set the universe in motion with the power of His words and established the law of confession, but many believers have suffered needlessly by misunderstanding the power of their words. As you begin to change the words you speak, you will rewrite their future and revolutionize your life.

5. **THE TONGUE – A CREATIVE FORCE**
   by Charles Capps

   Words are the most powerful things in the universe! God's creative power is still just as it was in the beginning of time when He stood there and said, "Light – be," and light was. His Word spoken from your mouth and conceived in your heart becomes a spiritual force releasing His ability within you. Learn to speak His faith-filled words to your situation and see your life transformed!

6. **THE VOICE OF JESUS**
   Speaking the Word of God with Authority
   by Leroy Thompson

   Break the cycle of powerless confession by putting faith-filled words to work in your everyday life. Readers will get this message: Words can change your world!

7. **THERE IS A MIRACLE IN YOUR MOUTH**
   by John Osteen

   Your miracle is in your mouth. Dare to speak those promises out loud. Say them to yourself! Say them to the devil! Confess them in the face of all contrary evidence! The Lord will surely make His promises come true in your life. When you SAY and CONFESS His Word, He brings the miracle to pass!

MASTER YOUR MONEY

A good man leaves an inheritance for his children's children.
Proverbs 13:22 NIV

1. A SEED WILL MEET ANY NEED
by Keith Butler

In this life-changing book, Bishop Butler will help you understand God's rules for victorious living. Scripture tells us that if we are obedient to God's voice, then His blessings will overtake us. If you have a need and the blessings of God have not overtaken you yet, find out what you may be missing.

2. I'LL NEVER BE BROKE ANOTHER DAY IN MY LIFE
Real Answers to Financial Hardships
by Leroy Thompson

Dr. Thompson shares real answers and insight through God's word on how to steer free from the traps and deception of the enemy and how to get from under the grips of financial bondage forever. As you apply these real solutions to your life, you will never be broke another day in your life!

3. INCREASE GOD'S WAY
by Jerry Savelle

Did you know that there is absolutely no way that you can walk with God, keep His covenant, and not experience financial increase? As you serve God and put His Word first place in your life, there should be signs of financial increase. It doesn't matter what your situation is right now, God wants and expects you to increase. And if you are not, it's a violation of spiritual law.

4. **PROSPERITY**
   Good News for God's People
   by Frederick K.C. Price

   Discover the many misconceptions about wealth that could actually be preventing you from getting wealth and living the life that God the Father created for you to live.

5. **RICH GOD POOR GOD**
   Your Perception Changes Everything
   by John Avanzini

   Understand that everything God puts in your control comes as a blessing so that you, in turn, can be a blessing. As you fulfill the desires of the Rich God by properly redistributing His wealth, you will access one of the most powerful keys to unlocking your personal financial success!

6. **THE BLESSED LIFE**
   The Simple Secret of Achieving Guaranteed Financial Results
   by Robert Morris

   This book will transform your life for the better, bringing you guaranteed financial results. But it will do more than that. It will change every area of your life: marriage, family, health and relationships. For when God changes your heart from selfishness to generosity, every part of your life-journey is affected.

7. **YOUR 10-DAY SPIRITUAL ACTION PLAN FOR YOUR COMPLETE FINANCIAL BREAKTHROUGH**
   by Kenneth and Gloria Copeland

   Whether you're facing financial turmoil or just wanting to live debt free, this interactive LifeLine kit contains an in-depth, 10-Day Spiritual Action Plan designed to help you think scripturally about your finances, wealth and prosperity.

Decide to Abide

*If ye abide in me, and my words abide in you,
ye shall ask what ye will, and it shall be done unto you.*
John 15:7 NIV

1. **GOD'S WORD: THE HOLY BIBLE**
   by *The Inspiration of the Holy Spirit*

   MATTHEW 6:33 AMP
   But seek (aim at and strive after) first of all His kingdom and His righteousness (His way of doing and being right), and then all these things taken together will be given you besides.

2. **8 WAYS TO CREATE THE LIFE YOU WANT**
   The Anatomy of a Successful Life
   by *Creflo Dollar*

   There are proven steps that can lead you to the life you want. Learn the comprehensive and practical applications that you can apply to your daily life and achieve all that God has predestined for you.

3. **GOD'S MASTER PLAN FOR YOUR LIFE**
   Ten Keys to Fulfilling Your Destiny
   by *Gloria Copeland*

   God has a master plan for your life. Discover the 10 keys for finding your destiny. Living a godly life is within your reach no matter your age, your background, your past sins or your current circumstances.

4. **LIVING LIFE ON TOP**
   Winning Over Life's Challenges
   by *Keith Butler*

   If you're experiencing stresses socially, physically, or financially, be encouraged! God has provided everything you need to live life with courage. GOD HAS MADE A WAY!

5. **MAXIMIZE THE MOMENT**
   God's Action Plan for Your Life
   by T.D. Jakes

   Using biblical principles that reveal the keys to personal success available to every one of us, Bishop Jakes teaches that every moment of every day, God provides all we need to achieve that success. He explains how to release ourselves from damaging relationships and move beyond our painful pasts.

6. **YOUR BEST LIFE NOW**
   7 Steps to Living at Your Full Potential
   by Joel Osteen

   In this straightforward guide, Joel Osteen gives you a way to improve your life for good and help you experience victory, joy, and satisfaction every day.

7. **YOU'VE ALREADY GOT IT!**
   So Quit Trying to Get It
   by Andrew Wommack

   This book is filled with the good news that God's response isn't based on the things you must do; it's based on what Jesus did. As you read, you'll gain the knowledge to trust God. It's only the truth you know that will set you free!

* *MASTER YOUR MONEY BONUS*

*The resources above provide a spiritual foundation;
the resources below provide practical application.*

1. ### THE TOTAL MONEY MAKEOVER
   A Proven Plan for Financial Success
   by Dave Ramsey

   7 organized, easy-to-follow steps that will lead you out of debt and into a Total Money Makeover. Plus, you'll read over 50 real-life stories from people just like you who have followed these principles and are now winning with their money. It is a plan designed for everyone, regardless of income or age.

   ### THE TOTAL MONEY MAKEOVER WORKBOOK

   With inspiring real-life stories, thought-provoking questionnaires, and inventive exercises that really do exercise your spending and saving habits, this workbook will help you literally work out your Total Money Makeover.

2. ### FINANCIAL PEACE REVISITED

   How to become debt free with Dave's simple Debt Snowball method; learn the truth about debt that you won't hear from any other money "experts."

   ### FINANCIAL PEACE PLANNER

   Assess the urgency of your situation; understand where your money's going.

3. ### MOMENTUM: BUILDING THE KINGDOM DEBT-FREE

   Momentum is a workshop that teaches church leaders how to cultivate a culture of generosity. Churches will learn how to handle God's money God's way while reaching out and making an impact on the community.

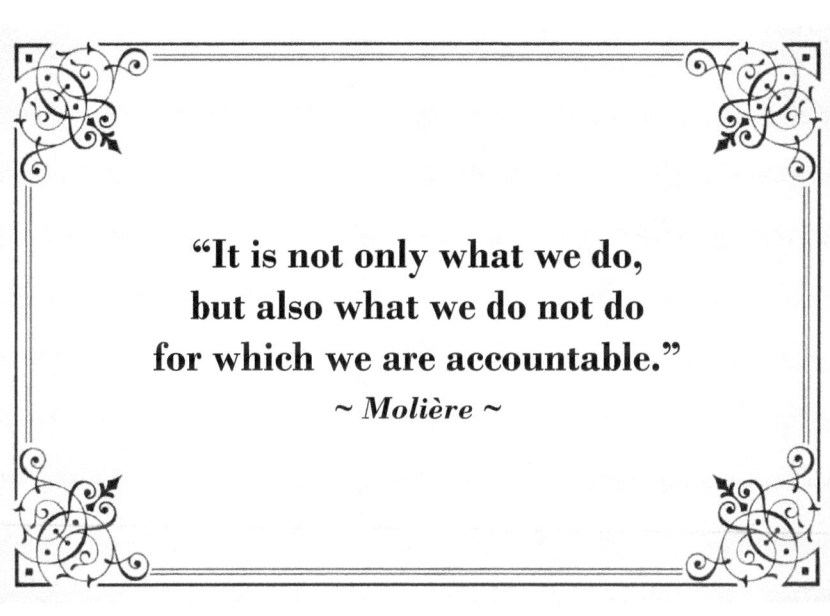

About The Author
D AWN J OYNER

"Every sunset brings the promise of a new dawn"

The essence of this statement is exemplified in the life of **DAWN JOYNER** – wife of *Christopher Joyner*, mother of *Brian, Katrina, Tyrique & Little Chris* and grandmother of *Cassidy* – an anointed singer / songwriter / musician / entrepreneur / author and motivational speaker who evangelizes the message of God's Love through the Ministry of Music and Multimedia.

Born and raised in Brooklyn, New York, Dawn began her music ministry at the tender young age of two when she performed *"The Lord's Prayer"* during divine worship service. Since that time, Dawn has been actively developing and honing the musical gifts God has blessed her with.

Dawn's speaking and writing gifts began to flourish in 1997 when the Holy Spirit impressed her to form *Phenomenal Woman Ministries,* an international ministry that encourages and empowers women to be diligently instrumental in preserving and restoring their families in accordance with Proverbs 14:1 - *"A wise woman builds her home."*

While living in New York, Dawn began facilitating monthly motivational *PrimeTime Forums* designed to esteem, enlighten and entertain the Phenomenal Women God placed in her life. After relocating to Atlanta in 2007, the PrimeTime Forums were replaced by *Powerful* Prayer & Praise Conference Calls where weekly she ministers to women under the anointing of the Holy Spirit.

Dawn's burning passion to share with the people of God what the Spirit of God has shared with her manifests through her music ministry and her speaking and writing gifts that edify and minister grace to the hearers.

All glory and honor belongs to El Elyon, the Most High God, for the great things He has done in the life of…

D AWN J OYNER

FROM OVERDRAFT TO OVERFLOW
3 Steps to Possession in a Recession

Copyright © 2010 by Déjà MultiMedia Group LLC
All rights reserved.

www.ingramcontent.com/pod-product-compliance
Lightning Source LLC
Chambersburg PA
CBHW070638160426
43194CB00009B/1493